GCSE

REVISION

RESCUE

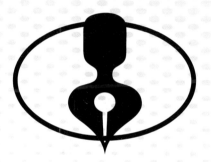

ENGLISH

**Steve Eddy and
Ruth Coleman**

Hodder & Stoughton

A MEMBER OF THE HODDER HEADLINE GROUP

The Authors and Publisher are grateful to the following for permission to reproduce copyright materials: page 45 Crisis, the national charity for single homeless people, page 47 Independent (UK) Newspapers Ltd., page 61 Atlanta Duffy, page 64 Random House Ltd., page 72 Grace Nichols from *The Fat Black Woman's Poems*, Little Brown. Other illustrations are taken from the authors' own title, *Revise GCSE English* also published by Hodder & Stoughton.

A catalogue record for this title is available from the British Library.

ISBN 0340 775 696

First published 2000

Impression number 10 9 8 7 6 5 4 3 2 1
Year 2005   2004   2003   2002   2001   2000

Editorial, design and production by Hart McLeod, Cambridge

Printed in Spain by Graphycems for Hodder & Stoughton Educational, a division of Hodder Headline Plc, 338 Euston Road, London NW1 3BH

Contents

Revision Rescue   4

Literary Prose 1   7

Structure of literary prose   7
Character   9
Style and language   11
Setting and atmosphere   13
Plot and structure   15
Themes   17
Viewpoint   19
Comparing texts   21
Literary Quiz   23

Non-fiction 2   24

About non-fiction   24
Letters   26
Diaries and journals   28
Biography and autobiography   30
Travel writing   32
Information   34
Non-fiction Quiz   36

The Media 3   37

About the media   37
Facts, opinions and argument   39
Bias   40
Comparing media   42
Advertising and appeals   44
Presentation   46
Media Quiz   49

Drama 4   50

Background   50
Style and language   52
Character   54
Social and historical context   56
Themes   58
Performance   61
Plays versus prose fiction   62
Considering a scene   64
Drama Quiz   65

Poetry 5   66

About poetry   66
Poetic form   68
Language and poetic devices   70
Studying poems   72
Applying what you know   74
Comparing poems   75
Poetry Quiz   77

Drafting, Proofreading and the Exam 6   78

Improving a first draft   78
Sequencing and paragraphing   79
Punctuation (1)   80
Punctuation (2)   82
Spelling (1)   84
Spelling (2)   86
Commonly confused words   87
Tackling the exam   89
Answering questions   90
Drafting Quiz   94
Answer to sequencing exercise   95
Sample Mind Map   96

The pages that follow contain a gold mine of information on how you can achieve success in your exams. Read them and apply the information, and you will be able to spend less, but more efficient, time studying, with better results.

This section gives you vital information on how to remember more while you are learning and how to remember more after you have finished studying. It explains

- how to use special techniques to improve your memory
- how to use a revolutionary note-taking technique called Mind Mapping that will double your memory and help you to write essays and answer exam questions
- how to read everything faster while at the same time improving your comprehension and concentration

Your amazing memory

There are five important things you must know about your brain and memory to revolutionise your school life.

1 how your memory ('recall') works while you are learning

2 how your memory works after you have finished learning

3 how to use Mind Maps – a special technique for helping you with all aspects of your studies

4 how to increase your reading speed

5 how to zap your revision

1 Recall during learning – the need for breaks

When you are studying, your memory can concentrate, understand and remember well for between 20 and 45 minutes at a time. Then it needs a break. If you carry on for longer than this without one, your memory starts to break down! If you study for hours non-stop, you will remember only a fraction of what you have been trying to learn, and

you will have wasted valuable revision time.

So, ideally, study for less than an hour, then take a five- to ten-minute break. During the break listen to music, go for a walk, do some exercise, or just daydream. (Daydreaming is a necessary brain-power booster – geniuses do it regularly.) During the break your brain will be sorting out what it has been learning, and you will go back to your books with the new information safely stored and organised in your memory banks.

2 Recall after learning – the waves of your memory

What do you think begins to happen to your memory straight after you have finished learning something? Does it immediately start forgetting? No! Your brain actually increases its power and carries on remembering. For a short time after your study session, your brain integrates the information, making a more complete picture of everything it has just learnt. Only then does the rapid decline in memory begin, and as much as 80 per cent of what you have learnt can be forgotten in a day.

However, if you catch the top of the wave of your memory, and briefly review (look back over) what you have been revising at the correct time, the memory is stamped in far more strongly, and stays at the crest of the wave for a much longer time. To maximise your brain's power to remember, take a few minutes and use a Mind Map to review what you have learnt at the end of a day. Then review it at the end of a week, again at the end of the month, and finally a week before the exams. That way you'll ride your memory wave all the way to your exam – and beyond!

Amazing as your memory is (think of everything you actually have stored in your brain at this moment) the principles on which it operates are very simple. Your brain will remember if it:

(a) has an image (a picture or a symbol);

(b) has that image fixed

(c) can link that image to something else.

3 The Mind Map® – a picture of the way you think

Do you like taking notes? More importantly, do you like having to go back over and learn them before exams? Most students I know certainly do not! And how do you take your notes? Most people take notes on lined paper, using blue or black ink. The result, visually, is boring! And what does your brain do when it is bored? It turns off, tunes out, and goes to sleep! Add a dash of colour, rhythm, imagination, and the whole note-taking process becomes much more fun, uses more of your brain's abilities, and improves your recall and understanding.

A Mind Map mirrors the way your brain works. It can be used for note-taking from books or in class, for reviewing what you have just studied, for revising, and for essay planning for coursework and in exams. It uses all your memory's natural techniques to build up your rapidly growing 'memory muscle'.

You will find sample Mind Maps at the end of this book. Study them, add some colour, personalise them; and then have a go at drawing your own – you'll remember them far better! Put them on your walls and in your files for a quick-and-easy review of the topic.

How to draw a Mind Map®

1 Start in the middle of the page with the page turned sideways. This gives your brain the maximum room for its thoughts.

2 Always start by drawing a small picture or symbol. Why? Because a picture is worth a thousand words to your brain. And try to use at least three colours, as colour helps your memory even more.

3 Let your thoughts flow, and write or draw your ideas on coloured branching lines connected to your central image. These key symbols and words are the headings for your topic.

4 Then add facts and ideas by drawing more, smaller, branches on to the appropriate main branches, just like a tree.

5 Always print your word clearly on its line. Use only one word per line.

6 To link ideas and on different branches, use arrows, colours, underlining and boxes.

How to read a Mind Map®

1 Begin in the centre, the focus of your topic.

2 The words/images attached to the centre are like chapter headings, so read them next.

3 Always read out from the centre, in every direction (even on the left-hand side, where you will have to read from right to left, instead of the usual left to right).

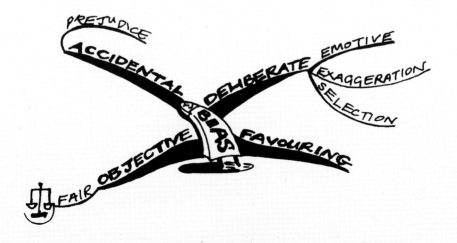

4 Super speed reading

It seems incredible, but it's been proved – the faster you read, the more you understand and remember! So here are some tips to help you to practise reading faster – you'll cover the ground more quickly, remember more, and have more time for revision!

First read the whole text (whether it's a lengthy book or an exam paper) very quickly, to give your brain an overall idea of what's ahead and get it working. (It's like sending out a scout to look at the territory you have to cover – it's much easier when you know what to expect!) Then read the text again for more detailed information.

Have the text a reasonable distance away from your eyes. In this way your eye/brain system will be able to see more at a glance, and will naturally begin to read faster.

Take in groups of words at a time. Rather than reading 'slowly and carefully' read faster, more enthusiastically. Your comprehension will rocket!

Take in phrases rather than single words while you read.

Use a guide. Your eyes are designed to follow movement, so a thin pencil underneath the lines you are reading, moved smoothly along, will 'pull' your eyes to faster speeds.

5 And finally...

Have fun while you learn – studies show that those people who enjoy what they are doing understand and remember it more, and generally do it better.

Use your teachers as resource centres. Ask them for help with specific topics and with more general advice on how you can improve your all-round performance.

Personalise your Revision Rescue by underlining and highlighting, by adding notes and pictures. Allow your brain to have a conversation with it!

Tony Buzan

How to use this book

Revision Rescue:English is clearly divided into subject chapters and topic sections. Each contains the facts you need to know, with key words highlighted for extra clarity.

The tinted boxes contain useful tips and hints, words and ideas to remember and short quizzes to test your knowledge and highlight areas that you may need to revise again.

Each chapter ends with a longer quiz related to the topic covered.

The Exam Emergency Service on Teletext

As you revise, you can boost your knowledge even further with a free exam emergency service on Teletext.

At key revision times, this service offers subject-specific advice, tips and hints for effective exam performance and guidance for planning you revision... until the very last minute! You will find a wide range of subject quizzes, which change regularly so you can test your knowledge again and again.

Literary Prose 1

1

Coverage: character; style and language; setting and atmosphere; plot and structure; themes; viewpoint; comparing texts.

Structure of literary prose

Character

- What are the main characters like?

- Does something happen to a character as a result of his/her personality?

Style and language

- Writer's style – descriptive or economical?

- Easy or difficult to read?

- Words used – familiar or unfamiliar?

- Sentences – short or long?

Setting and atmosphere

- Where are scenes set? Weather 'mood'?

Plot and structure

- Is the action more or less important than what a character learns?

- Does the action lead on to the next event/incident?

- Are clues planted?

- How does the author start/finish the story?

Themes

- What ideas are explored by the writer?

- How is the theme presented – directly/indirectly; imagery; irony?

Viewpoint

- From whose point of view is the story told?

Structure of literary prose – Mind Map

Getting into a novel

- Read the cover 'blurb' for an idea of what to expect.

- Dip into the first chapter and read bits at random.

- Scan the first chapter for character names. Write them down.

- Skim the first few paragraphs for their broad sense.

- Start reading more closely. Re-read the opening if your mind wanders.

- Be an active reader. Ask yourself questions, e.g. about characters.

- Make character Mind Maps.

Character

Imagine a story without characters. Although some works have been written from the point of view of animals, e.g. *Watership Down*, we are usually offered a human character to engage with. Think about:

Impressions

- How is the **main character** described?
- What does the character say and do?
- Mind Map or note descriptive details that help to create a full picture of the character.
- What are the character's circumstances – e.g. privileged and spoilt; poor and oppressed?
- Does the impression change as the novel develops – e.g. Darcy in *Pride and Prejudice*?

Minor characters

- Why are they there?
- Do they reveal something about a main character?
- Are they part of a sub-plot?

Sympathy/empathy

Does the writer want us to sympathise with, or step into the shoes of, a particular character? If so, how is this achieved? For a good example, look at Charles Dickens's description of Charley, a minor character in *Bleak House* (Chapter 15). Other characters make **observations** about Charley, **describing** her home, the relationship she has with the brother she cares for, and **giving details** of her courage.

Do you find yourself desperately caring about a character/knowing how the character feels? How does the writer achieve this response?

Colloquial writing

Colloquial language is ordinary and familiar rather than formal. It can be used to develop character and give conversations a local flavour. It can also make comments about social class, a lack of education, or add humour. Look at Laurie Lee's excuses to avoid lessons from *Cider with Rosie*:

'I dunno, miss; you never learned us that.'
'I 'ad me book stole, miss...'
'Please, miss, I got a gurt 'eadache.'

Emotions and attitude

- Does a character reflect the beliefs and opinions held when the work was written?

- Does a character reflect the beliefs and opinions of the writer?

- Try listing what each character in a scene is feeling.

- Language and tone used – what effect does this have on you, or on other characters?

- What ideas and attitudes are displayed by the character?

- Do we like/respect the character and so agree with him/her?

- Do we think the character's ideas are as ridiculous as the character that has been presented?

Relationships with other characters

- Where character clashes occur, what effects do they have?

- How is the conflict or contrast between characters presented?

Compare Bathsheba's suitors in *Far from the Madding Crowd* and the conflict arising between them. Or, look at Edgar and Heathcliff in *Wuthering Heights*. What can you find out about Bathsheba and/or Catherine from what they **say**, **think** or **do** in relation to their suitors?

Practice

From memory make as many statements as you can about a character you are studying. Use these statements to make a Mind Map.

Think about the novel

Help yourself to revise a particular book with these questions:
- What kind of novel is it?
- How does the title reflect the content?
- Can you give a brief summary of the story?
- What might the author have been hoping to achieve?
- How did the writer hold your attention?
- What is distinctive about the book or the writer?
- Why would you recommend it (or not) to other readers?

Style and language

Style is the way a writer makes words work together to tell a story. This tone, the voice of the writer, is as individual as a person's handwriting. The nuts and bolts of style include choice of words, figures of speech, type of sentence, paragraph, dialogue, imagery, irony and humour. The author's background may also influence style, and autobiographical material may be included.

Begin by asking yourself if a book is so enjoyable that you forget you're reading – or not!

Words

- Old-fashioned or modern; if it is difficult to understand – work out the general meaning of the phrases.
- Odd order of words – try putting the sentence into your own words.
- Many adjectives (descriptive) or few (economical)?

Sentences

If long, break up into separate parts. Semi-colons (;) do the job for you, conjunctions (e.g. *and*, *for*) join parts of sentences together.

Dialogue

- A lot or a little.
- Complexity – articulate person or simple, uneducated person.
- Informal/slang, or formal (typical of late Victorian style; e.g. Dickens).
- Type – legal jargon; written in accent; long or short exchanges.
- Action and thoughts developed through conversations (i.e. dramatic, like a play).

Foreshadowing

Clues given to warn of what's to come.

Style

Ernest Hemingway typically used short sentences in the form of statements. This reflected his earlier journalistic writing. He believed that such writing was true to experience and avoided the use of more decorative, or literary writing.

Hemingway's simple words and sentences were carefully ordered, however, and his careful use of literary devices such as imagery and irony made his work original for its time.

Images

What word pictures does the writer use to make an idea come alive? What images are used to make comparisons between things, or to show the importance of an emotion a character is experiencing?

Symbols – does the writer use something 'concrete' to represent something abstract – e.g. scales to represent justice?

Irony

A device in which what is said is opposite to what is meant. For example, when something turns out in the opposite way to that which was intended as if fate were mocking those involved. Check whether there is any difference between what's said and what's meant.

Humour

How is funny prose achieved? Look at the description of the characters; inappropriateness of some action or gesture; embarrassing behaviour; misunderstandings; devices such as similes and when something is likened to something else in an amusing way.

 Practice

1 List the challenges you have come across in the style of a writer you are studying.

2 Write about or Mind Map what it is about the style of a writer that held your attention.

Dish of the day – description

Ingredients
Literary devices
Several different-coloured pens and highlighters:

Method
- Circle the adjectives (describing words), e.g. the ⟨playful⟩ kitten.
- <u>Underline</u> images (word pictures).
- **Highlight** the similes, e.g. skin like ancient parchment.

Take careful note of the effect made by these devices and how they combine. Do they complement or curdle? What effect does this have on your literary palate?

Setting and atmosphere

Descriptions of places and settings set the scene and create mood and atmosphere. Always look at the **details of description** and pick out **specific words**, particularly **adjectives**. Also look at the **overall effect**. Are there **sights**, **sounds** or **smells** that contribute to mood?

Where

Rural settings – often suggest innocence and purity. The title *Far from the Madding Crowd* suggests slow, peaceful country life away from the bustle and worry of cities. **City settings** mean sophistication and immorality – this often comes up in the novels of Jane Austen.

Landscape – wild moors in *Wuthering Heights* are threatening, foreboding and reflect wildness of emotion in Heathcliff and Cathy.

Descriptions of **rooms** or **buildings** can set the scene and prepare us for the kind of story to come; e.g. *The Fall of the House of Usher* by Edgar Allen Poe.

Weather/elements

These can create a sense of **danger**, **trouble**, or **conflict**; e.g. a thunderstorm brings Mary Shelley's *Frankenstein* alive with impact and foreboding. Rain can set the right tone for a character to be glum.

Light and **dark** – create mood or make a point. When Curley's wife enters the bunkhouse and blocks the light in *Of Mice and Men*, we are warned of trouble to come. Sudden brightness can indicate that the character has learned something or resolved some difficulty.

Setting and emotion

Thomas Hardy's *Tess of the D'Urbervilles* provides a good example of the way that authors use setting to create atmosphere and a sense of fate.

An innocent Tess is first presented in an open valley, her seduction takes place in old woodland, and her love affair is conducted in a summertime garden. Her later desolation is reflected in a barren landscape, and she is ultimately sacrificed on the altar stone at Stonehenge.

Time/history

Is the story set in the past, the present, or the future? Is the cultural attitude linked to the date? In *Staying On* by Paul Scott, old age and an old way of life track each other. In *Brave New World* by Aldous Huxley, there are no moral dilemmas about sex and reproduction.

Practice

1 Look at Charlotte Brontë's description of Thornfield Hall after Jane Eyre leaves (Chapter 28). Here is a Mind Map of her experience.

2 Now describe or make a Mind Map of a car journey on a foggy night with a set of circumstances in the driver's life which echo the setting and atmosphere.

Humour in novels

Why is this funny?

Her smile wilted at the edges like the thirsty old plant she kept meaning to water.

The author uses the simile (comparing two things which are different, yet similar in some way) to create an image of the similarity between the droopy plant and the smile fading away.

Contrasting images which have something in common can make amusing pictures and contribute to atmosphere.

Plot and structure

Plot is the way events, incidents and characters are organised. Good plots sustain interest and perhaps create suspense. Some works have a **sub-plot** – a minor chain of events/actions which coincides with the main action, often echoing the main plot. Always look for clues and ask yourself the following:

• why did that happen?
• why is this happening?
• what will happen next and why?

Sustaining interest

How is your **attention** captured and held? In *The Woman in White* by Wilkie Collins, reader attention is fixed on a character and an increasingly exciting chain of events. Then, the focus shifts to a different set of events and a different character's view of what's going on. You want to read on to find out what happens – suspense!

Suspense – what follows is uncertain, but you want to know. Were the events expected or unexpected – did they take a dramatic turn? Consider how suspense drives plot. In pre-1900 prose fiction, chapters often ended on an exciting note to make readers buy the next issue of a serial magazine story.

Sense of unity – you won't feel satisfied unless all loose ends have been tidied up. If any part of a good plot is taken away, its unity will be broken up.

Twist – an unexpected turn of events or a revelation which changes things.

When you write about literary prose...

Do
• Trust your judgement.
• Express your own fresh ideas in your own words.
• Remember that quality is always more important than quantity.
• Support what you say with examples and/or quotations.
• Give attention to detail.
• Refer to other relevant texts.
• Order your ideas into a clear sequence.

Don't
• Recycle copied information.
• Just retell the story.
• Ramble on.

Structure

This means the framework in which the plot is anchored – the interdependent balance between the different parts. Structure also applies to chapters and perhaps parts.

- **Sequence** – things must happen in the right order – most novels have a sequence, often with a clear beginning, middle and end.
- **Cyclical** – John Steinbeck's *Of Mice and Men* starts and ends in the same place, stating that everything will go on as before – characters are powerless to change anything.
- The **flashback** is another way to introduce and/or round off a novel. This technique can have the advantage of reassuring a reader that a character comes out of mortal danger unharmed. For example, L P Hartley uses the flashback in *The Go-Between*.

Practice

1 To help you understand the key elements of a plot try filling in the main events in a grid like this:

What?	Who?	When?	Where?	Why?

2 Think about the structure of a novel you are studying – is there a clear beginning, middle, end? Are cycles or flashbacks used?

Writing about writing

It is important to state more about what a writer is doing in a novel than simply asserting that 'the writer is saying or doing this or that'.

The following words may be used to comment more exactly on the precise job done by a piece of writing and can enhance the quality of your own response:

explain	involve	inform	persuade	describe	analyse
narrate	explore	argue	entertain	imagine	instruct

Themes

Themes are the **ideas** explored in novels. For example, the **subject** of George Orwell's *Animal Farm* is the way a group of animals behave with each other, but its central **theme** is comment and observation on world politics.

Common themes

- Human experiences (e.g. love, hate, conflict).
- Characters coming to terms with changed circumstances; learning from experience or resolving dilemmas.

Culture and convention

- Beliefs at the time of writing and setting; e.g. love themes are linked to marriage in novels written before 1900 – living together would have been scandalous.
- Novels (especially pre-1900) often carry a moral message from an author – everyone gets what they deserve; e.g. Fanny Price in *Mansfield Park* by Jane Austen.

How themes are developed

Consider how themes are developed by characters, through language, style, setting, atmosphere, plot, structure and viewpoint. For example, the theme of loneliness is central to Steinbeck's *Of Mice and Men*. The characters' lifestyles are lonely, the loneliest character whines like a pining dog when left alone and George plays card games on his own.

Practice
Use the Mind Map over the page as a model for the themes in a novel you are studying.

Symbols

Writers often use symbols to illuminate ideas in their novels.

In *Lord of the Flies*, William Golding uses a conch shell as a symbol of harmony, order, and the natural beauty of the remote island. As the novel develops, the conch is compared to a horrible pig's skull, reflecting the deterioration of both the boys' behaviour and the island's beauty.

What symbols are used in a novel you are studying?

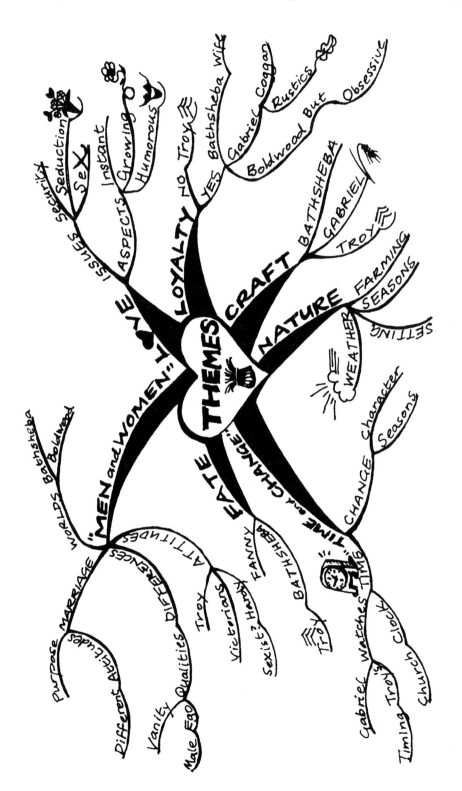

Viewpoint

The viewpoint is the outlook from which the events in the story are told. There are three main kinds:

Omniscient

Here the writer is everywhere, like a fly on the wall. The writer has access to everyone's thoughts and emotions and can switch between locations freely. Examples: *Of Mice and Men* by John Steinbeck and *Brave New World* by Aldous Huxley.

First person narrative

Events are told by **one character** from his/her point of view – 'I thought this or that'. This means that we only have his/her opinion or version of events. Usually, we like this character. Examples include: *David Copperfield* by Charles Dickens and *Jane Eyre* by Charlotte Brontë.

Sometimes we dislike, but develop sympathy for, the character who is telling the story. When this happens, the author has deliberately chosen to use such a viewpoint to make us react to him/her. Examples include: *Lolita* by Vladimir Nabokov and *The Collector* by John Fowles.

Sometimes first person narrative is used in an unusual way. Examples include: *The Go-Between* by L P Hartley where the narrator is a powerless child; and *Wuthering Heights* by Emily Brontë – related by Nelly, a minor character. In *Jane Eyre*, Charlotte Brontë's main character, Jane, addresses the reader directly:

'*Reader, I married him*' (Chapter 38).

Contrast and viewpoint

Look at these opening lines:

It was love at first sight. (*Catch 22* by Joseph Heller)
This is the saddest story I have ever heard. (*The Good Soldier* by Ford Maddox Ford)

In both cases we are drawn into the novel and want to know what will happen next. The author has captured us in the opening sentence. The emotions expressed in these examples are, however, in direct contrast. From what viewpoint is each told?

Third person

Here the story is told in relation to one main character. We do not read about the inner thoughts and feelings of other characters. Examples include: *Pride and Prejudice* by Jane Austen and *The Good Terrorist* by Doris Lessing.

Variations

Shifting viewpoint – sometimes several first person narratives are used together. Examples include: *Bleak House* by Charles Dickens and *The Woman in White* by Wilkie Collins.

Letters can also be used as a type of narration to advance the action.

Practice

1 Pick up a novel, and flick through it until you can say from what viewpoint it has been written.
2 Make a Mind Map of, or describe how, the viewpoint in a novel you are studying affects the way the story develops.

Viewpoint – Mind Map

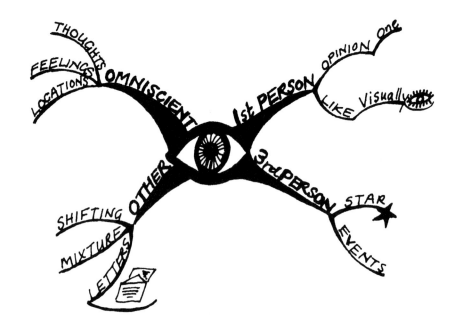

Comparing texts

Look for **similarities** and **differences** in the way characters are presented, in style, language, setting, atmosphere, plot, structure, themes and viewpoint. A useful starting point is to compare the way two stories begin, followed by a look at the middle and ends. In addition to those, look at:

Culture and convention

• Different cultures – obvious differences, similarities.

• Way of life, customs, language usage; e.g. American slang, Irish dialect.

• Descriptions of things, people, sights, sounds and smells.

Time of writing

How do writers reveal when they have written their work?

• Compare differences in the way characters behave – the lessons they learn, if any.

• The type of words and language used – use of dialogue, slang or formal English.

• The type of sentences.

• Use of suspense.

• Descriptions of everyday things – how different writers present the same themes.

• Obeying conventions.

Types of literature

Can you give examples of some of these types of literature: gothic, journalistic, romantic fiction, science fiction, crime fiction?

Conventions and cultures

Novels reflect the values and attitudes of the times in which they were written.

It is a truth universally acknowledged, that a single man in possession of a good fortune, must be in want of a wife. (*Pride and Prejudice* by Jane Austen, 1813)

This introductory sentence is not only constructed in a way we would now consider old-fashioned, it also contains a 'truth' which is no longer universally acknowledged.

A comparison

The 20th-century American writer John Steinbeck exposed the poor conditions and hardships of life during the economic depression of the 1930s. This type of literature became known as **social realism**. Less than a century before, Charles Dickens explored similar ideas, exposing the harsh lives led by the poor of Victorian Britain. Both writers sought to present the truth, had a social conscience and wanted, through their writing, to be agents of change for the better. Here is a Mind Map to show the comparison.

Practice

1 List some of the differences you might find in literature written before and after 1900.
2 Choose two works of literary prose. In what ways are they similar or different? Which do you prefer? Make a Mind Map to show your ideas.

Conventions and cultures

Remember that all novels reflect the conventions and cultural backgrounds of the place and time in which they are set.

Take particular note of the different customs, traditions, rituals and beliefs that you come across and note their effect.

Some ideas and attitudes may seem strange to you. Most novels, however, deal with common human experiences and emotions such as love, jealousy and hate.

Literary Quiz

True or false?

1 An author's views are always the same as his or her character's.
2 The technique known as **irony** can be used when there is a difference between what is said and what is meant.
3 Novels written after 1900 generally use longer sentences than those written earlier.
4 Novels generally reflect the cultural attitudes and value systems of the place and time in which they are written.

Literature quiz

1 The term **viewpoint** refers to:
   (a) a vantage point for admiring the landscape;
   (b) the outlook from which the events in the story are told.

2 The term **first person** describes:
   (a) narration by one character from his/her point of view;
   (b) the first character to be introduced.

3 A **theme** is:
   (a) the subject of a novel;
   (b) an idea explored in novels.

Who wrote these novels?

1 *Animal Farm* – L P Hartley, George Orwell, Paul Scott
2 *Far from the Madding Crowd* – Thomas Hardy, Wilkie Collins, Vladimir Nabokov
3 *Wuthering Heights* – Charlotte Brontë, Emily Brontë, Jane Austen
4 *Of Mice and Men* – William Golding, Aldous Huxley, John Steinbeck
5 *Pride and Prejudice* – Jane Austen, Charles Dickens, Doris Lessing
6 *As I Walked Out One Midsummer Morning* – Edgar Allen Poe, Mary Shelley, Laurie Lee

Answers

Who wrote these novels?
1 George Orwell
2 Thomas Hardy
3 Emily Brontë
4 John Steinbeck
5 Jane Austen
6 Laurie Lee

Literature quiz
1 (b)
2 (a)
3 (b)

True or false?
1 False
2 True
3 False
4 True

Non-fiction

> **Coverage: types of non-fiction; letters; diaries and journals; biography and autobiography; travel; information.**

About non-fiction

You'll find non-fiction in **newspapers**, **packaging**, **advertising**, **timetables**, **statistics**, **leaflets**, **listings**, **fliers**, **spreadsheets**, **textbooks**, **notices**, **rulebooks**, small print – and that's before you think about other media such as **radio** and **television**.

Non-fiction serves a variety of purposes. The media keep us informed with **reports** and **descriptions** of places or events. Leaflets or adverts persuade us to buy or do certain things. We rely on **reviews** of films and books to help us decide if we want to see or buy them. We might consult an **encyclopaedia** for information. We learn to distinguish between what is invented and what is non-fiction, and what is fact and what is opinion.

Reviews

Reviews of films, plays, books, CDs, etc. should help you decide if you want to see, read or buy them. Good reviews will contain:

• **Facts**: full title, who by, where showing/when published, times and/or prices, theatre company/hardback or paperback.

• **Critical opinions**: what was good and why, what was poor and why.

Note: Positive suggestions for improvement are more constructive than scathing criticism if you want to earn respect and goodwill.

When we hear of someone's remarkable achievements, expertise or courage, we read their **diaries** or **letters**. Accounts of their lives or special abilities will be in the **biography** and **autobiography** sections of libraries and bookshops. If we want to explore a new interest or fix a car, we might look for a **manual**. Holidays might inspire us to read **travel books** and **brochures** or **guide books**.

Our ability to understand and produce non-fiction is an essential life skill.

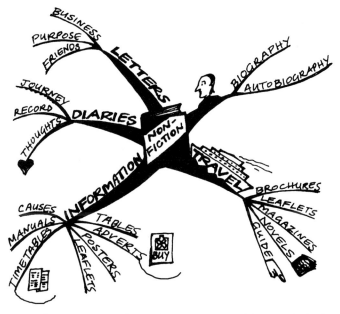

Here is a Mind Map of some types of non-fiction. You could extend the branches with examples of each type as you work your way through this section.

Instructions

Stick the egg in some hot water and boil for a while.

Good instructions should:

- assume little knowledge
- omit nothing apparently obvious
- contain a clear, concise, logical progression of steps towards completion. It usually helps to imagine that the reader is completely inexperienced.

Put the egg in a small pan, cover with water, bring to the boil, then turn down the heat and simmer for 3–4 minutes depending on preference.

Letters

Formal letters

- Set the letter out in a generally accepted manner.
- Use smart A4 sized paper.
- Use neat, legible handwriting, or type/word-process.
- Be clear, concise and polite, even if complaining.
- Use a new paragraph to introduce an idea.
- Use the language that fits the purpose and creates the right overall tone – the most difficult part.
- Some people find it easier to clarify their thoughts about something important if they write rather than talk to someone else.
- If you are replying to a letter and have been given a reference number, remember to quote it.
- You will often be asked to 'put it in writing' – remember that doing so is legally binding!

Pause and think about how a letter applying for a holiday job would vary from one written to a friend who has just moved away.

Your address
Postcode
Date

Their address
Postcode

Dear (title of addressee)

Re: if any

This is the 'contract' part of the letter. It could be a request, a complaint, an application, an invitation, an enquiry, a confirmation, a brief note, etc...

Yours sincerely

Signature (if used).
Your name, printed if signature used.

Persuasive letters

These often use language that conceals the real meaning, such as:

- I would like to invite you = I am going to try to persuade you.
- You will be automatically entered into a prize draw – it will cost you nothing = we want to entice you to take part.
- Very easy/simply/all you have to do = wants to give impression of easiness.

Persuasive letters are always polite, and often friendly and chatty in tone.

Look at this Mind Map which shows some of the **reasons for writing letters**.

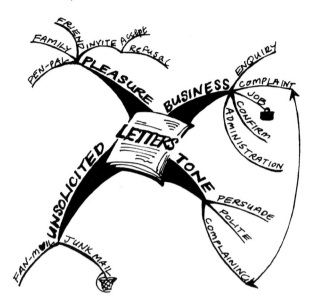

Practice

1 Write a brief letter which **politely** but **assertively** complains about an unsatisfactory purchase. Mind Map all the points you should include, such as what was bought, when, why it is unfit for the purpose, that you know your rights, and what you expect the addressee to do about it.

2 You have seen an advert offering a free place to the right person, to do something you have always wanted to do, e.g. go on safari. Apply persuasively, making sure you strike the right tone – selling yourself but not sounding big-headed!

Waffling on

Specialists sometimes use many words where a few would do:

The Draft Leisure Report was presented to relevant sub-committees and circulated for further comment in a consultation process to result in its amendment, ratification and presentation for approval, as the Leisure Report, at the Recreation Committee meeting to be held 30 November.

Or,

Following consultation on the draft document, the Leisure Report should be approved by the Recreation Committee, 30 November.

Diaries and journals

Here is a Mind Map of some **reasons for writing a diary**:

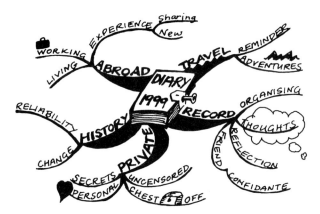

Features of diary-writing

- Usually personal so it can contain completely private information!
- Informal in tone.
- You can write what you like, ignoring all rules of grammar, punctuation etc.
- Likely to contain uncensored impressions, emotions, opinions.
- Written in the first person.
- Style – descriptive rather than economical.

Features of modern journals or logs

- Usually fact rather than opinion.
- Kept on ships and aeroplanes.
- Used on expeditions; e.g. mountain-climbing.
- May be written in note form.
- Not necessarily written in first person.
- Style – economical rather than descriptive.

Diaries and journals

What a vile little diary! But I am determined to keep it this year. (Katherine Mansfield)

It is refreshing to know that great writers failed to keep up their diaries because no-one checked that it was up-to-date.

Because they offer complete freedom, diaries can develop your skills in writing fact or fiction creatively. Try writing one without the watchful eye of family and friends – you will impress yourself!

Famous diaries

Diaries were often called journals in earlier centuries. Famous diaries are considered works of literature; they are often written by artists, writers and musicians. Diaries may reveal creative processes. For example:

• Virginia Woolf – used her diary to solve work-related problems.

• Lord Byron – his diary betrays a love of women, that he did most things in a hurry, and that he had problems with punctuation!

Some diaries provide important detail about historical events. For example:

• Samuel Pepys (17th-century Londoner) – a rare surviving account of everyday life in England.

• Ann Frank – a Jewish girl who hid from the Nazis in the Second World War.

Practice

1 *Star-date, captain's log* ... The TV programme *Star Trek* begins with these words. Describe as many situations as you can think of in which a journal or log would be written, and then write a sample entry for one of them.

2 Imagine you wake up one morning to find yourself stuck on a desert island. All you have is a notebook and a pen. Write a few days' diary entries including practical details, how you are feeling, and how you might get rescued.

Diaries and journals

Short-lived writer Katherine Mansfield (died at 35) wanted her journal to die with her. Some of it survived her, however. What it revealed of her unconventional life was not only considered shocking, but greatly influenced women seeking greater equality with men.

Should the record of her personal thoughts and feelings have been allowed to die with her? How would you feel about your diary being published after your death?

Biography and autobiography

Biographies

- Accounts of people's lives which they didn't write themselves.
- Subjects tend to be famous; e.g. royal family, writers, artists, politicians.
- Not always written with the subject's permission.
- There may be more than one biography of someone famous; e.g. members of the royal family have official biographers to create a censored account and to show the person in the most favourable light – omitting scandals.
- Two writers' accounts of the same event could differ!

Here is a Mind Map which could help plan a **biography of Diana, former Princess of Wales**.

Truth is stranger than fiction

Have you ever heard this said? It can be difficult to establish what is truth and what is fiction with diaries, journals, biographies and autobiographies.

Whilst diaries are essentially private records, usually containing the truth, this is not necessarily so with biographies and autobiographies.

Look at how biographers and autobiographers present someone's life, in particular:

- how they look back on incidents that occurred;
- how they analyse and present the attitudes that surrounded them.

Autobiographies

- Accounts of people's lives which are written by the subjects themselves.

- Can be written by ordinary people who become famous – perhaps they have led particularly difficult lives; are gifted in some way; or have overcome great hardship or oppression with unusual courage.

- May somehow typify an era.

- May be written with such an engaging style that the simplest details contain much to interest the reader.

- Some autobiographies are written by 'ghost writers' – their name does not appear on the published work – because the subject does not have enough skill to write their own story.

- May be so well written that they come to be regarded as literary works; e.g. Laurie Lee's *As I Walked Out One Midsummer Morning*.

Practice

1 Try Mind Mapping your ideas about biographies.
2 Think of an incident or event in your life which sticks out in your mind. Write a page of your autobiography recording this incident or event in a way which will amuse, entertain or engage a reader. Making a Mind Map of the factors involved and how they relate to one another may help you to get started. Ask your teacher if you can include this task in your coursework.

Techniques for reading non-fiction

Skimming: for general content. Note headings, illustrations, paragraph beginnings and endings.

Scanning: for key features; e.g. people in news.

Speed reading: to understand and remember more.

- Skim whole book, exam paper etc. before closer reading.
- Don't hold text too close to your eyes.
- Take in groups of words at a time (not single words).
- Use a pencil or pen under the line to guide you.

Travel writing

Features

- Popular type of non-fiction.

- Not necessarily well-written.

- Often adventurous or something unique – biggest, first, only person to...

- It is the author's particular explanation of travels which interests us.

As a major world industry, travel and tourism agencies also generate literature promoting their destinations.

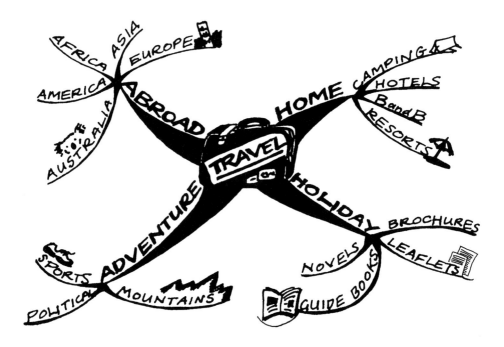

Travel writing in history

Before technology brought swift means of transport, travel writing tended to be concerned with the discovery and description of places and peoples the reader was unlikely to encounter in person.

As fewer places in the world are left unvisited, travel literature increasingly features the undertaking of the unusual – cycling around the world, walking through hostile desert. Is this true of any travel writing you have read?

Examples

The language and style of travel writing depends very much on its **purpose** and **audience**. Compare these two descriptions of Delhi, India where there is an old and modern part of the city:

(a) *Delhi. Capital of Kingdoms and empires. Now, a sprawling metropolis with a fascinating blend of the past and the present. A perfect introduction to the composite culture of an ancient land. A window to the kaleidoscope that is India.*

Leaflet from India Tourist Board, London.

(b) *Delhi is a fantastic place, fascinating and filthy in the extreme. Old Delhi is full of snake charmers, bear wrestlers, opium dens and dead bodies lying in the gutter. But New Delhi is beautiful, modern, airy, green and lush. Amazing.*

Letter from 16-year-old schoolboy to his parents – *On the Road Again*, Simon Dring, BBC books, 1995.

Quotation (a) emphasises Delhi's importance, gives little detail and uses persuasive words to create a romantic impression rather than providing facts. Its **purpose** is to entice the reader – **audience** – to visit India.

Quotation (b) concentrates on the feel of the place, with actual details of who and what the boy found there, rather than dealing with historical context or its relative importance as a city. The quotation contains contrasts; it is not trying to 'sell' the city (dead bodies). Its **audience** is private – fitting to the letter it comes from.

1 Pick out one fact and one opinion from each description of Delhi.
2 Write a short piece that would be suitable for a tourism brochure. Then write another piece about the same place as a paragraph from a short story.

Types of travel writing

These statement are taken from (a) a guide book, (b) a personal account of a journey, (c) a railway company's promotional literature. Decide which is which.

Hints: subject, awareness or not of the writer, accuracy, fact or opinion.

- *The station also boasts the architecturally impressive Brunel bar.*
- *I left the station and headed in what I hoped was the right direction for town.*
- *The railway station is situated one mile from the town centre.*

Information

When looking at leaflets and adverts, try to:

• distinguish between fact and opinion

• comment on the impact; content; language; layout and presentation

• think about how the material persuades; sells or argues a case.

You will boost your marks if you can comment on the language and devices used to deliver the information.

Language and devices

Ask yourself these questions:

Impact: bright and 'pick-uppable' or dull and boring? Zany or conventional?

Title/headings: catchy, jokey, puns? Too long, too short? Do they stand out and grab your attention – e.g. capital letters, larger size of print, use of colour and different typeface?

Content/language: does it tell you too much, too little? Is it easy to understand or too technical? Does it play on emotions (pick out specific words or phrases to back up opinion)? Has it got long or short sentences? Is it punchy or sloppy? Is the information source biased or neutral? Is it giving facts or opinions?

Presentational devices: are there questions and answers; listed points; speech bubbles with pictures of celebrities or 'a person in the street' approving a product or cause? Written by an 'invisible' expert? Any boxes; tables; sections or gaps? What effect do these devices have? What is the overall tone?

Pictures and captions

How true are these sayings?

'A picture is worth a thousand words.'
'Every picture tells a story.'
'The camera never lies.'

In your own non-fiction you may use words to create images in the reader's mind. A carefully selected picture that has something to say may do the work for you.

A caption is not always necessary but, if used, should confirm the reader's understanding of the picture.

Practice

1 Write a paragraph which gives two sides of an issue of your choice without betraying where you stand.

2 Imagine you have the job of **preparing a leaflet to help people stop smoking**. Use the ideas in this Mind Map to help you make up a brief for a designer. Describe what the leaflet should contain, and how it should look. Include information about the style, language and techniques you could use, and add brief suggestions for titles, pictures and layout.

Sales and packaging

Office Stores is changing its image. You will be writing the copy (text) to be printed on boxes containing computer discs.

Which of these slogans might you use and why?

- Back up your data/Store your stuff/Whisk the disc.
- No 1 office supplier – with discounts/Biggest and best budget store.
- Top quality assured/100% certified and error free/Tested and guaranteed – or your money back.

Non-fiction quiz

Fact or opinion?

Which statement from each pair below would be acceptable in a **fact sheet** on genetic modification (GM)?

1 (a) The use of GM is questionable.
   (b) GM is totally unacceptable.
2 (a) GM will definitely affect the well-being of the food chain.
   (b) GM may affect the well-being of the food chain.
3 (a) Further trials into the safety of GM are needed.
   (b) GM is completely safe.

True or false?

1 Diaries are usually private places meant only for oneself to read.
2 It is possible to write non-fiction creatively.
3 Biographies are written by the subject him or herself.
4 Encyclopaedia entries should be comprehensive and unbiased.
5 Non-fiction should only deal with facts.
6 Personal opinions are not acceptable in reviews.
7 When issuing instructions it is best not to assume prior knowledge.

Sponsorship appeal

You intend to cycle across Africa for a charity. The only problem is that you need sponsorship. Put the following points in order as you might arrange them to be included in an appeal letter:

(a) exactly what equipment/fares you need sponsorship for
(b) details of your route
(c) brief summary of whole project
(d) why the charity should be supported
(e) appeal for the money
(f) some facts about you.

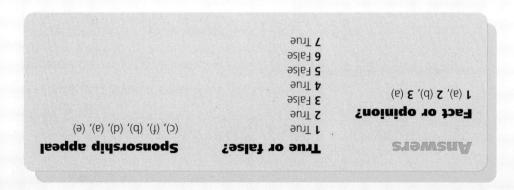

Answers

Fact or opinion?
1 (a), **2** (b), **3** (a)

True or false?
1 True
2 True
3 False
4 True
5 False
6 False
7 True

Sponsorship appeal
(c), (f), (b), (d), (a), (e)

Coverage: facts, opinions and argument; bias; media comparisons; advertising and appeals; presentation.

About the media

In your exam, you may have to comment on a newspaper or magazine article, or on an information leaflet or brochure. You are less likely to be asked about radio, television, film or advertising. However, these could well come into your coursework. Consider:

• the difference between fact and opinion and how both are used in an argument

• how the form of different media affects their content

• how 'emotive language' and reasoned argument are used to persuade

• presentational devices – e.g. pictures and graphics, captions, headlines

• how advertising and other forms of appeal persuade.

You probably know more than you think about these subjects. Make a Mind Map of what you know, then compare it with the one on the next page.

When studying the media be aware of two things:

• purpose: what a media item is trying to achieve – e.g. to entertain, persuade, inform or sell

• target audience: who it is aimed at – e.g. style-conscious teenagers, or middle-aged men with money to spare.

Media keywords

Tabloid Small-format newspaper, e.g. *Sun*; aimed at less educated readers than **broadsheets**, so easier to read, with less space given to serious news.
Broadsheet Large-format newspaper; e.g. *Guardian*; aimed at more educated readers interested in serious news.
Layout Design of a paper or magazine, including typeface, headline size etc.
Press release Information offered to the media; e.g. by a company about a new product.
Leader Newspaper article openly giving **opinions** about a news story.

Media – Mind Map

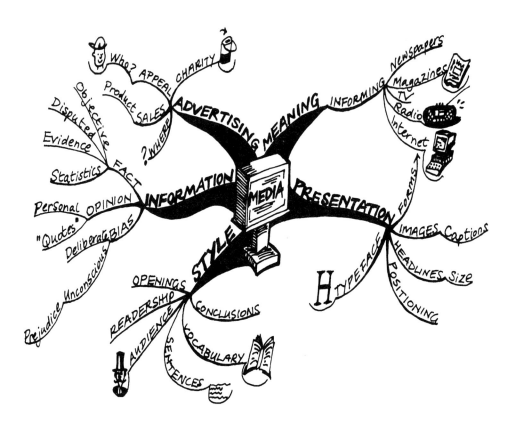

Media vocabulary

Jargon Specialist language used by those knowledgeable about a subject. Often found in specialist magazines.

Cliché Phrase used so often that it is boring; e.g. *at this moment in time*.

Buzzword Fashionable word or phrase for popular concept; e.g. *accountability*.

Euphemism Word or phrase used to make an unpleasant fact seem acceptable; e.g. *economical with the truth*, or *relieved of her duties* for 'sacked'.

Facts, opinions and argument

Facts and opinions

Facts are statements of information which can be proven to be true, or which are generally agreed. For example:

• the Moon has no light of its own

• tigers are carnivorous

• Michael Owen has played football for England.

Opinions express a point of view, or a judgement:

• moonlight is very romantic

• we should do more to protect tigers

• Michael Owen is England's greatest footballer.

Facts can be disputed, e.g. in court. Sometimes they appear to change, e.g. as a result of scientific discoveries.

Argument

An argument is an opinion backed up by factual evidence and reasoning. Use colours to mark facts, opinions and arguments in the following example:

The number of tigers surviving in the wild is decreasing every year. This is because of human population increase, the destruction of forest habitats and the hunting of tigers, especially so that their bones can be used in Chinese traditional medicine.

Unless we do more to enforce international restrictions, tigers will be extinct in the wild by the year 2015. This would be a tragedy for several reasons: the tiger is a noble and beautiful animal, and the world would be poorer without it; humans still have a lot to learn about tigers; tigers play an important role in forest eco-systems; they also encourage the tourist trade in some countries. Above all, we have a moral duty to protect all the species of the world.

Read a newspaper 'Leader comment' or 'Editorial'. Use different colours to mark facts, opinions and arguments. Hint: for arguments, look out for phrases like 'so', 'because', 'therefore' and 'as a result'.

Bias

Objectivity and bias

To be **biased** is to favour one person, group of people or viewpoint over another, regardless of the facts. A sports referee should never be biased, nor should a judge. A media report shows bias when its presentation of facts is influenced – deliberately or not – by opinion or prejudice. An unbiased report is called an **objective** one. It is generally agreed that news reporting should be objective.

Deliberate and accidental bias

Deliberate bias comes in many forms; e.g. **political propaganda** either changes the facts or presents them in a way that favours one political group. Compare:

In only six months the government has succeeded in fulfilling half of its election promises.

Six months have passed and yet half of the government's election promises remain unfulfilled.

Is there any difference in the facts presented here?

Accidental bias is caused by **prejudice**, when speakers or writers are unaware of how their views colour the way they present facts.

Gender discrimination

- Some people call women *girls* – even though they would not call men *boys*.
- It is usually possible to avoid using *man* for 'person'; e.g. *Humans are descended from apes.*
- There are no gender-free pronouns for *he/she* and *his/her*. Some people accept *their*; e.g. *Ask your friend for their opinion.* It is safer to reword; e.g. *Ask for your friend's opinion. Ask your teacher for his or her opinion.*

Techniques of bias

When bias is deliberate there are several techniques used to present facts persuasively:

Emotive language aims to produce an emotional response. Examples include:

- environmental protesters might be called eco-warriors, hippies or trouble-makers
- a government might 'slash' lone parent benefit, or 'claw back' money in taxes.

Exaggeration:

- can use adjectives – e.g. 'colossal', 'gigantic', 'minuscule' or 'negligible'
- or imagery – e.g. 'United wiped the floor with the City players'.

Selection:

- includes only those details that fit the chosen viewpoint
- quotations may seem objective but may be biased in their selection or used out of context.

Bias – Mind Map

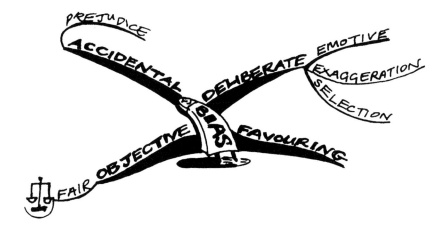

Practice

1 Note emotive language in charity appeals.
2 Compare coverage of the same political event in two different newspapers.

Comparing media

Differences

It makes no difference whether you listen to news on the radio, watch it on TV or read it in the papers – right? Wrong. Here's why:

- each medium (singular of 'media') presents information differently; this affects its content – and our experience
- different media can do different things.
- news is not just information – it's also entertainment: it has to win an audience to earn licence money or advertising revenue
- the media play to their strengths – a major news story with no interesting pictures will get less TV coverage than a less important story with exciting pictures.

Pros and cons

Radio – no pictures, but its technology is fairly simple, so it's cheaper than TV and can report sooner. In an emergency, all it needs is a reporter with a mobile phone. Reporters can also interview passers-by, and have studio debates or discussions, including phone-ins.

Television – has pictures but it has to hold the viewers' attention, and so cannot spend too long on any one story. Some stories are important but visually dull – e.g. the collapse of a big financial institution. Television is good on 'human interest' – it can film interviewees. Faces and gestures convey more than words alone.

Newspapers – are less immediate: they have to be typeset, printed and distributed. But they can use more words, because readers can take their time and select. Many papers are now on the Internet, updated hourly.

News features

You may be asked to comment on a news feature.
A typical format for these is:

1. What, who, where, when, why?
2. How? More details
3. Extras, quotes

Example: (1) Bomb, IRA, London, last night, retaliation; (2) Van, stolen from car park; (3) Many injured; 'It was complete chaos ...'

Look out for opinions in the choice of words; e.g. *The thugs who did this ...*

Magazines – may have articles about the news, but as they are published weekly or monthly they are most likely to discuss long-running stories or subjects of current interest. The main aim of many is to entertain.

Magazine markets

Every magazine is aimed at a specific readership, determined by:
- age group; e.g. teen, 20-something, middle-aged
- gender – male, female or both
- socio-economic bracket - based on values, education and spending-power
- special interests; e.g. outdoor pursuits, knitting, rock music
- ethnicity – a few are aimed at an ethnic community.

Their language will reflect this; e.g. *luscious superhunk* in a teen-girl magazine, or technical jargon in a computer magazine.

Media Choice – Mind Map

Practice

1 Which media would you choose to catch up on the latest news (a) on a train; (b) driving a car; (c) at home after a hard day? Why?
2 Compare coverage of a news event on radio and TV, and in a paper. To do this, video the TV news, record the radio news, and buy the paper the next morning. Compare the number of words, the information given, and the techniques, e.g. quotations, interviews, pictures.

Advertising and appeals

Advertising must **get our attention**, **be memorable** and **persuade**.

Attention-grabbers

- Shock – e.g. 'Rats – they're closer than you think' (with a rat close-up).
- Colour and sound – direct sensual appeal.
- Arresting images – e.g. a fish on a bicycle.
- Questions – e.g. 'What's the **guaranteed** way to get a good GCSE English grade?'
- Sex and romance.

Memory

It's more important to be memorable than to be convincing. Some attention-grabbers are memorable by appealing to our senses, by portraying unusual images or by using sex. Others are:

- humorous – especially puns
- stories – especially with a punchline
- puzzles or mysteries – hold the attention longer
- slogans – short, cleverly worded messages, often rhyming; e.g. 'You can with a Nissan'
- jingles – musical slogans.

Techniques of persuasion

- Claiming value or effectiveness.
- Image – suggesting that if you buy the product you'll be like the people in the advert (cool, clever, rich, sexy).
- Guilt or insecurity – 'Don't you want the best for your kids?'; 'Can you be sure about your breath?'

Advertising, poetry and memory

There *is* a link between these three – one you should understand and use:

- Advertising only works if it's memorable.
- Memory works by making connections – e.g. between two visual images.
- A poetic image combines two ideas, stimulating our imagination and memory.
- Rhymes link two or more words, making them easier to remember – whether you're a bard reciting an epic, or someone hearing an advertising slogan.

Targeting

Adverts are aimed at particular groups of people – determined by age, sex, attitudes, interests, self-image etc. This is their **target audience**. Magazines and radio and TV programmes are also targeted. Advertisers use magazines and TV programmes with the same target audience as their product.

Charity appeals

Both businesses and charities use language and images to **persuade**. They often use **emotive language**.

Look at the Crisis advert. Comment on: the caption's Christmas joke; the boxed insets in the illustration; the focus on 'Mary'; what feelings the line 'Could you sleep easy ...' plays on.

Will you give Mary a bed this Christmas?

24 DAYS TO GO
0°c LAST NIGHT

At 16, Mary ran away from a life of abuse. Today she is homeless. Could you sleep easy on Christmas Eve knowing she was shivering in a bus shelter?

You can help keep Mary, and thousands of vulnerable people like her, safe and warm over Christmas. With £25 from you, Crisis can provide a warm bed, hot meals, clean clothes and someone to talk to at one of our shelters.

As the days count down to Christmas, over 2,000 homeless people are counting on Crisis. We're counting on **you**. Our service depends on public donations. So

Emotive language

The words *motion*, *motive*, *emotional* and *emotive* are connected. *Emotive* language plays on your *emotions* to set you in *motion*. It *motivates* you.

When an appeal begins *Life is tough for a baby elephant*, the word *baby* gains our sympathy.

If a bomb victim appeal shows a picture of a boy without hands, captioned *Turning the page isn't so easy for him*, we feel lucky to have hands, and guilty if we turn over.

Presentation

Presentation is how a written message is presented. In your exam you may be asked to comment on this. Note:

• use of images (pictures) with words – photos, drawings, graphics

• placing – where on a page a news item or other text appears

• type – size and style.

Front page news

Look at the front page of *The Independent* on the next page, and the numbered notes below.

1 **Advertisement for paper:** tries to make you buy the paper by telling you what it includes – TV Guide etc.

2 **Main story:** editor's choice of a story to front the paper, positioned at the top of the page to show its importance. Headline is large (in tabloids it may fill most of a page) – it's meant to strike us and make us buy. Often includes emotive language: 'fear', 'revolution', 'go ... now' etc.

3 **Photographs:** accompany stories to catch our attention.

4 **Secondary stories**: smaller heading shows editor considers them less important than the main story. Front pages often include a 'fun' story near the bottom of the page. The headline is often jokey, as it is in the bottom story here.

5 **Follow-up:** previewing other articles related to main news.

6 **Contents:** useful in broadsheet papers.

7 **Advertising:** a source of income for papers. Advertisements target the paper's readership.

Words and pictures

Advertisers and layout artists understand that words and pictures can work together to give a more powerful image than either of them alone.

Captions can direct the way in which we interpret a photograph. Sometimes different newspapers use the same picture with captions that interpret it in quite different ways.

Headlines or any other highlighted or large text can also influence how we interpret information. Compare headlines in different papers.

Front page news

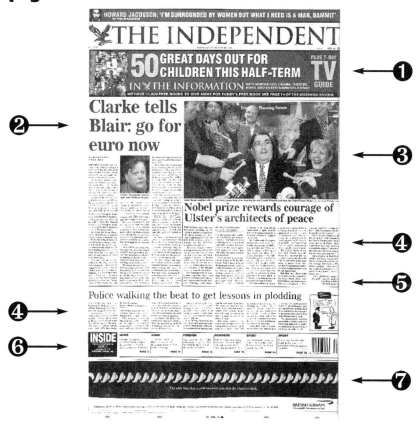

Practice

Make an A4-sized plan of the main presentational features of a newspaper's front page – as shown above. Use the spaces on your plan to make notes on these features.

Information sheets

You may be asked to comment on an information leaflet. You will be asked to assess and explain its effectiveness.

Consider **who** it is aimed at, and **why** they need the information. Consider the style and level of **language** used. How difficult is the **vocabulary**? Are **technical terms** used? Is any technique (e.g. humour) used to make it memorable?

Finally, how do pictures and type enhance the overall effect?

Jargon

Jargon is specialist language used by those who are knowledgeable about a subject, or who wish to appear so. It is often found in specialist magazines.

Some people use it because they want to be seen as part of a group whose image they like, e.g. surfers, computer experts, or skateboarders.

The more positive use of jargon is to express concepts that would otherwise take more words to explain.

Off-side

One area in which it is easy to spot bias is sports reporting:

Liverpool played a blinder of a game, to the delight of an appreciative crowd. Gibbs and Johnson held the mid-field against all Nottingham's assaults, while Davies and Grimm darted in between their defenders with speed and daring. Their crowning moment was Grimm's last-minute goal, slipped past a powerless defence. Score: Nottingham 3 Liverpool 1.

Letters

If asked to write a 'letter to the editor' in response to a news feature or leader (giving the paper's opinion), you will get marks for:

• coherent argument, fluently expressed, including appropriate vocabulary
• appropriate **register** – in this case fairly formal standard English
• varied and correct sentence structure
• paragraphing that reflects the sequence of ideas
• reasonable spelling and punctuation
• using correct letter layout.

Letter layout

The Editor
Wapford Echo
13-14 Knoll Road
Wapford WA3 7JK

33 Stain Street
Wapford
WA1 3BB

4 April 1999

Dear Editor

Blah, blah, blah

Yours sincerely

Jason Tiler

Media quiz

Fact or opinion?

1 The Second World War ended in 1945.
2 Teenage crime should carry stiff penalties.
3 Over 60 per cent of children worldwide live below the poverty level.
4 Foxes sometimes kill chickens.
5 The world would be a better place if we were all vegetarians.
6 There are more women than men in the world.
7 Studies indicate that most people want to keep the monarchy.
8 Women are more caring than men.

What words describe:

(a) specialist language used by those knowledgeable about a subject?
(b) a fashionable word or phrase for a popular idea?
(c) a phrase used to make something seem more acceptable?
(d) the design of a paper or magazine?
(e) favouring one person, viewpoint, country etc. over another?
(f) an article giving opinions about a news story?
(g) an over-used phrase?
(h) a small-format newspaper?

Bias

1 What techniques of bias are used here?
   (a) These brutes represent an open sore on the flesh of our society;
   (b) Manchester were 3-0 up before Arsenal even knew the game had begun;
   (c) Hitler raised national pride, ended unemployment and introduced youngsters
   to healthy outdoor living.
2 What abstract noun is used for the opposite of bias?
3 What adjective describes language that plays on our emotions?

Answers

Fact or opinion?
1 fact
2 opinion
3 opinion
4 fact
5 opinion
6 fact
7 fact
8 opinion

What words describe:
(a) Jargon
(b) Buzzword
(c) Euphemism
(d) Layout
(e) Bias
(f) Leader
(g) Cliché
(h) Tabloid

Bias
1 (a) Emotive language
   (b) Exaggeration
   (c) Selection
2 Objectivity
3 Emotive

Drama

Coverage: background; style and language; character; social and historical context; themes; performance plays versus prose fiction; considering a scene.

Background to Shakespeare

First some basics, then read the Mind Map on the next page, before working on the rest of the topic.

The Elizabethan theatre

Try to see a performance of the play you're studying. Visit the New Globe Theatre, London, if possible. Remember the following about Elizabethan theatre:

• little scenery; no lighting effects; the scene had to be set largely by the words – sometimes with the help of music

• female roles were played by boys – one reason why they have relatively few lines (though there are important female roles)

• audiences were rowdier than now – people drank beer and ate during the performance, and many were standing

• comedy (comic relief in tragedies) was sometimes used to hold an audience.

Types of play

Shakespeare wrote four types of play:

• **Comedies** – featuring humour, confusions, disguise, happy endings (usually marriages); no deaths.

• **Tragedies** – centred on a tragic hero (or couple) whose downfall and death through error and fate win our sympathy (e.g. *Romeo and Juliet*).

• **Histories** – based on historical characters and conflicts.

• **Romances** – 'problem' plays featuring magic, mystery, morality and unlikely happy endings (e.g. *The Tempest*).

Practice

1 Mind Map the differences between the Elizabethan theatre and its modern equivalent.

2 Decide which type of play you're studying. How do the play's characteristics emerge?

3 Copy the Mind Map below, using colour. Add to it as you work through the chapter.

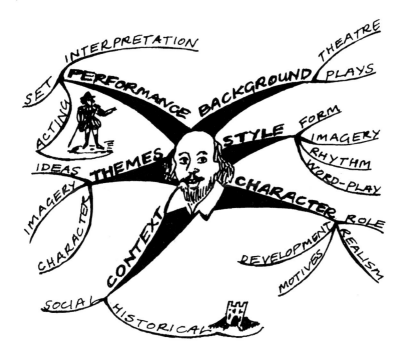

Appreciating Shakespeare

You should be able to comment on four main aspects of the play: **plot and structure**; **character**; **themes**; and **language**.

Try to see the play as a whole. Every Shakespeare play shows a situation in which social harmony is disrupted by events or by the desires and behaviour of the characters.

By the end of the play the situation is resolved and order is restored. Consider how this occurs in the play you're studying.

Style and language

Poetry and prose

Shakespeare's plays include poetry (verse) and prose (no rhymes or fixed line-lengths). Commoners speak in prose. Nobles use it only informally – or if mad. Note, too, that Shakespeare had to appeal to all ranks of society, so his language is sometimes simple, sometimes sophisticated.

Shakespeare used 'blank verse' – i.e. non-rhyming verse. It usually has five pairs of syllables to a line, with stress on each second syllable. It is also called **unrhymed iambic pentameter** (Greek *pente* = five). Some speeches end with a rhyming couplet.

Imagery

Images are word pictures describing a character's behaviour, or something abstract – like love – as if it were something tangible. Shakespeare uses four types of imagery:

- **Similes** compare two things: *It seems she hangs upon the cheek of night/ As a rich jewel in an Ethiop's ear* (*Romeo and Juliet*, Act 1, scene 5); normally include 'like' or 'as'.

- **Metaphors** describe a thing as if it is something else: *Life's but a walking shadow* (*Macbeth*, Act 5, scene 5).

- **Comparisons** measure one thing against another: *As violently as hasty powder fir'd/ Doth hurry from the fatal cannon's womb* (*Romeo and Juliet*, Act 5, scene 1).

- **Personification** describes something as if it were a person: *The gray-ey'd morn smiles on the frowning night* (*Romeo and Juliet*, Act 2, scene 3).

Images match themes

Romeo and Juliet contains contrasting images of light and dark, suggesting both love's hopefulness and the family hatreds that threaten the lovers.

Romeo sees Juliet as a *bright angel*; she sees him as *whiter than new snow upon a raven's back*. He describes the family tomb in which he finds her dead as a *palace of dim night*.

Note how images match themes in the play you're studying.

Word music

Shakespeare fits rhythm to sense. A downcast Macbeth sees a bleak, monotonous future: *Tomorrow, and tomorrow, and tomorrow* (Act 5, scene 5). The sound of words is important, too, especially alliteration – repetition of a sound – usually at the beginnings of words; e.g. *big-bellied with the wanton wind* (*A Midsummer Night's Dream*, Act 2, scene 1).

Word-play

Shakespeare excels at using the **pun**: the use of a word with two meanings, or of two similar-sounding words, where both meanings fit in different ways; e.g.

Mercutio: ... *dreamers often lie.*
Romeo: *In bed asleep, while they do dream things true.*
(*Romeo and Juliet*, Act 1, scene 4)

Shakespeare also uses **oxymorons** (opposites); e.g. *O heavy lightness, serious vanity ... Feather of lead, bright smoke, cold fire, sick health* (confused Romeo, Act 1, scene 1).

Practice

1 Read some blank verse aloud. Tap out the syllables, counting them on your fingers. Try speaking in blank verse.

2 Note all the images in one Shakespeare scene. Identify what type they are. Consider why they are appropriate for the subject they describe, and how they match the theme of the play.

Shakespeak – tips on language

Focus on **who** is speaking, the general sense of **what** they say, and **why** they say it. Check the **mood**. Does rhythm or imagery suggest an emotion?

Notice word choice; e.g. the simplicity of Prospero's lines in *The Tempest* as he prepares to surrender his powers: *We are such stuff/ As dreams are made on; and our little life/ Is rounded with a sleep.*

Read in sentences, not lines: a sentence may continue beyond a line-end.

Character

Many Shakespeare characters are psychologically realistic, but they also have a **dramatic** purpose; e.g. *Romeo and Juliet* would not be a tragedy but for Juliet's strict father. Some characters are types: villains; authority figures; jokers; lovesick lovers and foolish lords.

Checklist of character *X*

- How realistic is *X*, and how realistic is *X* **meant** to be?
- What is *X*'s dramatic role?
- What are *X*'s motives and problems?
- How does *X* develop?
- How do you feel toward *X*?
- What can be said for and against *X*?

Another way to explore a character is with a Mind Map – the one on the next page is a basic structure for you to extend.

In the exam ask yourself the questions above, concentrating on those most relevant to the exam question. Use quotations to support what you say. If asked to write **in character**, imagine how it would feel to be the character at the set point in the play.

Practice

1 Note phrases revealing character traits in the first and last speeches of a major character. How has he/she developed?
2 Practise 'hot-seating' with a partner. Take it in turns to be a character while your partner asks questions; e.g. 'How did you feel when ...?', 'What are your worries ...?' etc.

Dilemmas

Much of the dramatic interest in Shakespeare is provided by **dilemmas**: characters are pulled in different directions by conflicting desires.

Macbeth wants to become king, yet feels deeply what a sin it would be to murder his king – who is also his guest and relative – to achieve this. Juliet dreads taking the Friar's sleeping potion, but knows this is her only chance to be with Romeo.

What dilemmas feature in the play you're studying?

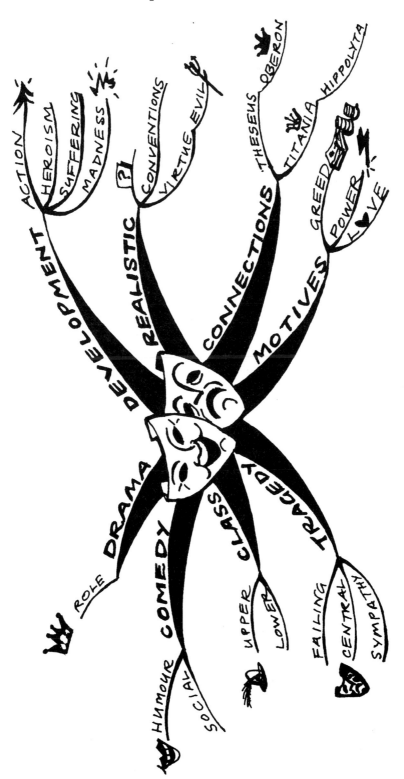

Social and historical context

In GCSE English you will be expected to know about social and historical context. Shakespeare is probably the oldest literature you'll study, so you need to make a special effort here.

What is context?

Much of what you read in Shakespeare is timeless. His themes – love, hate, greed etc. – are still as relevant as ever. His characters have the same motives and weaknesses as we do. However, some things have changed and need to be understood. Social context refers to the general attitudes of the time, e.g. the belief that women should always obey their husbands. Historical context refers to specific historical facts or events that influenced Shakespeare.

Examples of key points for key plays

1 *Macbeth* (Act 2, scene 4 – Macbeth has murdered the King):

Old Man: *Tis unnatural,*
Even like the deed that's done. On Tuesday last,
A falcon, towering in her pride of place
Was by a mousing owl hawked at and killed.

Context: Macbeth flatters James I, Scottish-born King of England. James believed that kings were appointed by God. He (and most of the audience) would believe that killing a king – a crime against God and nature – would be echoed by unnatural events. The Elizabethans believed in the social order. For a king to be killed by a lesser man (Macbeth) would be like a falcon being killed by an owl.

Social context

During Shakespeare's time most Europeans still believed in God, but some questioned the meaning of life – especially whether we have **free will** or are ruled by **destiny**.

The class system was rigid – monarch and nobles at the top, peasants at the bottom. Shakespeare's plays assume that nobles are better than commoners.

Women had few rights and were expected to obey fathers or husbands. What power they had came from their sex appeal and persuasiveness.

2 *Julius Caesar* contains similar ideas, but emphasises the events as omens of things to come. The Elizabethans were more superstitious than us, and believed in fate and astrology. A historical point about *Julius Caesar* is that if Shakespeare wanted to explore the morality of killing a potential tyrant, it was politically safer to do it in the context of ancient history.

3 In **The Merchant of Venice** Shylock complains of Antonio:

He hath disgraced me and hindered me of half a million; laughed at my losses, mocked at my gains, scorned my nation, thwarted my bargains, cooled my friends, heated mine enemies! And what's his reason? I am a Jew!

Context: in Shakespeare's time Christians believed that money-lending for profit was immoral, yet they needed loans for trade. Other professions were closed to Jews owing to prejudice, so they became money-lenders. The Jewish doctor of Elizabeth I was accused of trying to poison her and hanged.

Practice

1 Research and Mind Map the social and historical context of the play you're studying.

2 Mind Map a plan for an essay on how you would relate the context of your play to the modern day. For example, the musical *West Side Story* was based on *Romeo and Juliet*.

Shakespeare (1564 – 1616): historical context

1580 Last 'miracle' play performance.
1583 Commercial expeditions to India and Persia.
1586 Tobacco introduced.
1587 Mary Queen of Scots beheaded.
1588 Spanish Armada defeated.
1592 Plague kills 15,000 in London – theatres shut.
1595 Spanish invade Cornwall; high heels for men.
1596 WC invented.
1600 Bruno executed for claiming Earth revolves round Sun.
1601 Earl of Essex executed for revolt against Elizabeth I.
1603 Elizabeth I dies. Succeeded by James VI of Scotland.
1605 Guy Fawkes plot.
1608 Telescope invented.

Themes

A theme is an important idea or subject explored in a play. If you are asked to focus on a play's themes Mind Map them and think about how they connect. The mini Mind Map below shows some of Shakespeare's themes. Which ones appear in the play you're studying?

Themes – Mind Map

Themes and character

Some characters are closely related to particular themes; e.g. in *Macbeth*, Macbeth himself is related to the themes of courage and time, Duncan and Malcolm to that of kingship. In *Twelfth Night* several characters represent aspects of the theme of love. In *Romeo and Juliet* the linked themes of love and hate are explored through the two main characters, and through their opposed families.

Themes and imagery

In some Shakespeare plays, themes are closely connected with imagery (see p. 51); e.g. in *Macbeth* characters are compared to animals. Macbeth likens himself to a bear tied to a stake. There is also imagery related to light and dark, and day and night, representing good and evil.

Practice

1 Mind Map the main themes of the play you're studying. For each theme, find a quotation that particularly relates to it.

2 Mind Map how one theme is explored through one major character. If possible, find images relating to both good and evil.

3 With a partner, roleplay a character being interviewed on a theme or two characters discussing a theme, e.g. Brutus and Cassius in *Julius Caesar* on fate and free will.

If music be the food of love …

Shakespeare often explores several aspects of a theme through his characters. In *Twelfth Night* he explores love.

Orsino is self-indulgently lovesick. Maria's affection for Sir Toby is rooted in reality. Malvolio and Sir Andrew show love's foolishness. Olivia falls for another woman – thinking her a man. Sebastian and Antonio demonstrate true friendship. Viola's love is patient and self-sacrificing.

Examine how characters demonstrate aspects of themes in the play you're studying.

Destiny

Shakespeare sometimes portrays life as being ruled by destiny, 'the gods' or 'the stars'; sometimes characters argue for free will.

Macbeth believes the Witches' prophecy that he will be king, and therefore murders Duncan. In *Julius Caesar* Calphurnia's dream anticipates Caesar's death. Hamlet comments that *There's a divinity that shapes our ends*.

Romeo and Juliet are *star-cross'd lovers* – doomed from the start. But in *Julius Caesar*, Cassius argues that men can be *masters of their fates:/ The fault ... is not in our stars ...* (Act 1, scene 2).

Prejudice

We cannot expect Shakespeare to defend minority rights quite as someone might today, but he does argue in favour of recognising what we have in common as human beings.

Romeo and Juliet shows the evil of hating someone for their family name; Shylock in *The Merchant of Venice* pleads that Jews are just like other people; Othello is English theatre's first black tragic hero.

How important is prejudice in the play you're studying?

Power

It is said that 'power corrupts'. This is true for many Shakespeare characters.

Macbeth kills for kingship, encouraged by his wife. In *Othello* Iago relishes the power he has to manipulate his master's emotions. In *The Tempest* Prospero loses his dukedom through seeking magical power, which he uses to rule Caliban and Ariel.

Even in the comedy *Twelfth Night* Malvolio attempts to wield power but is himself falsely imprisoned as a madman.

Performance

Elements of performance

Characters: how does the interpretation compare with how you see them? For example, Macbeth could be seen as a monster or a victim. Ask yourself how characters could have been played differently.

Acting: do actors fit their parts? Are they convincing? Do they put energy and meaning into the lines?

Set design: 'setting' – where the action occurs – is important in Shakespeare. A particular type of action and mood may be associated with each setting; e.g. *The Merchant of Venice* (Rialto – business, Belmont – love). Do the set and lighting reflect the mood?

Costumes: Elizabethan? Historically realistic? Modern? Do they reflect the characters and interpretation? Do they enhance the set? See the example costume below.

Music and sound: how are these used to create mood?

Updating: has the director tried to update the play or give it a new twist?

Blocking: the plan by which actors move around the stage – do they move appropriately? Do the positions reflect the relationships?

If you are considering a film, is it just a screen version of a stage production, or does it use realistic settings?

Practice

1 Make labelled costume sketches – like the one on the right – for characters in the play you're studying. Make notes on your costume choices.

2 Consider how the play you're studying should be produced. Make a Mind Map, using the headings given above.

Costume design for Phebe in 'As You Like It'

Modern drama – plays versus prose fiction

How is drama different from prose fiction?

- No description – e.g. scenes, characters – except by characters.

- No author commentary on events or characters' thoughts/feelings.

- Drama has limitations – e.g. hard to show an underwater diving scene or to deal with rapid scene changes; but can have action-only – wordless – moments or even whole scenes.

- Characters appear on stage.

Remember

A play needs characters, a plot and structure – usually leading to climax and resolution. To characterise a play consider the following:

- Motivation – what do the characters want, love, hate, worry about?

- Relationships between characters.

- Delineation – how we learn about the characters; what they say and do and what others say about them.

- Development as the play unfolds.

Setting and atmosphere in drama

Setting means where a scene takes place. This contributes to the **atmosphere**; e.g. cheerful, gloomy, tense.

In *Hobson's Choice,* Act 3 takes place in Maggie's cellar – 'workroom, shop and living-room'. Its simple practicality reflects her character and marriage, but hot-house flowers hint at her warmth. Hence the atmosphere is down-to-earth but friendly.

Make a table or Mind Map of settings in the play you're studying, showing what happens where, and how this relates to atmosphere.

Practice

Use the Mind Map below to help you Mind Map the play you're studying.

Drama – Mind Map

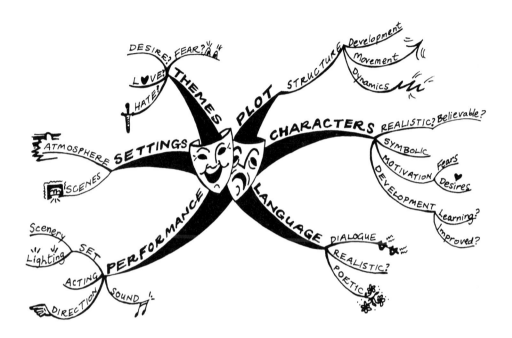

Themes in modern drama

Most of the themes in modern drama have been around for centuries: love, hate, greed, power, etc. However, some are new, or have taken on a new emphasis:

- The individual's response to social pressure; e.g. Miller, *A View from the Bridge*.

- Women's role in society; e.g. Brighouse, *Hobson's Choice*.

- Individual conscience and social responsibility; e.g. Priestley, *An Inspector Calls*.

- Class; e.g. Shaw, *Pygmalion*.

Considering a scene

You may be asked to comment on a scene in a play. You must try to look beyond the lines, to what is really happening. What are the characters thinking and feeling? What are their relationships? How would you stage the scene?

The passage below is from Arthur Miller's play *The Crucible* (Act 1, p. 48 in Penguin edition). It is based on true events which occurred in America in 1692, when several teenage girls were accused of witchcraft. Miller wrote the play in 1953, at the height of anti-Communist hysteria, when many leading intellectuals and people in the arts were imprisoned for their 'Communist sympathies'.

At this point in the play, suspicions of witchcraft are mounting. Some girls have been seen dancing around a fire in the forest, one of them naked. One girl, Betty, has fallen into a trance. Abigail, their leader, is questioned by Hale, an 'expert' in detecting witchcraft. Parris is the local vicar, Putnam a wealthy landowner. Abigail accuses the black servant, Tituba:

ABIGAIL: *She comes to me every night to go and drink blood!*

TITUBA: *You beg me to conjure! She beg me make charm –*

ABIGAIL: *Don't lie!* [To HALE]: *She comes to me while I sleep; she's always making me dream corruptions!*

TITUBA: *Why say you that, Abby?*

ABIGAIL: *Sometimes I wake and find myself standing in the open doorway and not a stitch on my body! I always hear her laughing in my sleep. I hear her singing her Barbados songs and tempting me with –*

TITUBA: *Mister Reverend, I never –*

HALE: [resolved now]: *Tituba, I want you to wake this child.*

TITUBA: *I have no power on this child, sir.*

HALE: *You most certainly do, and you will free her from it now! When did you compact with the Devil?*

TITUBA: *I don't compact with no Devil!*

PARRIS: *You will confess yourself or I will take you out and whip you to your death, Tituba!*

PUTNAM: *This woman must be hanged! She must be taken and hanged!*

Practice

1 What are the relationships between the characters? Draw a diagram to show their relative power in the scene. How would you show this on stage?
2 Why do you think Abigail accuses Tituba? Who do you believe? What questions would an audience be asking at this point?
3 A dynamic has been set up. Abigail has shifted the focus of blame from herself to Tituba. How must Tituba feel now? What might she do?
4 Write a scene based on this one, but set in a modern school.

Drama quiz

Shakespeare

1 Shakespeare's female characters have relatively few lines because:
   (a) women were supposed to be seen but not heard;
   (b) they were played by boys;
   (c) Shakespeare did not like female actors.
2 Which of the following would you find in Shakespeare's **comedies**? (a) magic (b) disguises (c) deaths (d) marriages (e) historical characters; (f) mix-ups.
3 What always happens to tragic heroes?

Drama

1 Is 'blocking' (a) part of a stage set; (b) how actors move around; (c) spoiling the audience's view?
2 What words describe the following:
   (a) the stage scenery?
   (b) the point where the action comes to a head?
   (c) the sense of order being restored at the end of a play?
   (d) what drives characters' actions?
   (e) how characters change?

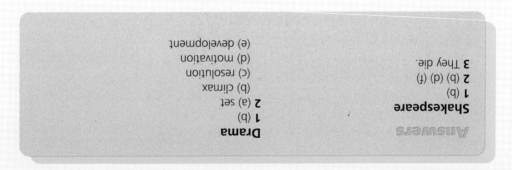

Answers

Shakespeare
1 (b)
2 (b) (d) (f)
3 They die.

Drama
1 (b)
2 (a) set
   (b) climax
   (c) resolution
   (d) motivation
   (e) development

Coverage: purpose; themes; form; language and poetic devices; studying specific poems; applying what you know; comparing poems.

About poetry

Purpose of the poem

Why has the poem been written? Is it **telling a story**? Is the poet **describing** something or offering you an **opinion**?

Themes

What is the poem about? Is this stated directly and obviously? Common themes are love, death, celebration, suffering, protest, childhood, thanksgiving, nature, time and reflections on life.

Format

What form does the poem take? Is it continuous or split into stanzas? Is line length the same or different?

Language

How do the words work together to make pictures, create a mood and present a satisfying piece of poetry?

The Mind Map on the next page summarises these points.

Practice

1 Skim read this topic to get a feel for studying poetry.
2 Apply the above to a poem you are studying. Discover something under each heading.

Getting into a poem

If you go blank at the sight of blank verse:

- look at the poem's title. What focus does it give to the text?
- read the poem several times
- read it aloud, trying out different tones, e.g. dramatic, funny, sad
- look for words and phrases which give you information about the subject and speaker of the poem
- look at the way the poem ends. Has it changed or developed?

Poetry – Mind Map

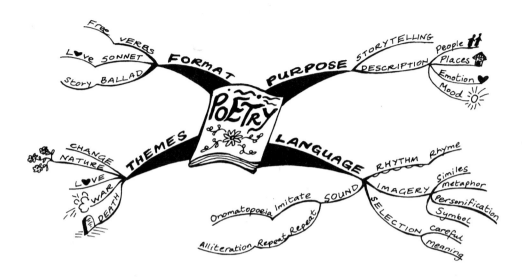

Lyric and narrative poetry

These terms are often used to describe poetry.

Lyric poetry is so called because it tends to use language which is considered imaginative, expressive or ornamental and song-like rather than factual, everyday and plain. Lyrical form is typically the sonnet, elegy (lament for the dead) or ode (addressing somebody or something).

Narrative poetry tells a story, typically in the form of an epic or a ballad.

Said or read?

The effect achieved by reading or speaking a poem can be strikingly different. The use of the repetition of sounds at the start of words (alliteration) in this extract is an example:

I caught this morning morning's minion, king-
dom of daylight's dauphin, dapple-dawn-drawn Falcon

    (*The Windhover* by G M Hopkins)

Try reading it aloud and silently. What do you notice?

Poetic form

Poetic form is the shape and structure of a poem, and the way (style) in which it's constructed, not what it's about. Elements include:

Rhythm – feeling of movement created by the balance between stressed and unstressed syllables. Here's a line from a poem written with a rap rhythm (read aloud and tap out the beats):

> *I wouldn't thank you for a Valentine* (Liz Lochead).

Rhyme – ordering of words or line endings to echo pleasing sounds.

• Complements and focuses the rhythm.

• Binds poem together and helps to amplify its meaning.

• 20th-century poetry often breaks the rules that earlier poetry followed.

Rhyming scheme – a pattern of rhyme at line endings; e.g.

> *Here I am, growing older,*
> *Thinking of poems*
> *To put in my folder*

Stanza – a group of lines of verse.

• Pattern depends on the number of syllables and how they are stressed.

• Separate stanzas often contain different thoughts or develop an idea.

• Sometimes they emphasise and repeat an important point.

• Stanza pattern can provide unity.

• Breaking such rules is more common in modern poetry.

Concrete poetry

Some poems take a format which reflects their theme or subject. The meaning of such poems is amplified by the shape.

Two of George Herbert's religious poems are *The Altar*, which is printed in the shape of an altar, and *Easter Wings* – a poem of two stanzas printed in the shape of a bird's wings.

Look at the work of e.e.cummings for other examples.

Couplets – two lines containing equal stress which end with rhyming words. Common before 1900, particularly to sum up in the last two lines (rhyming couplet).

Dramatic monologue – voice of a particular character narrating a poem, not the poet.

Epic – long narrative poem on a grand subject.

Sonnet – poem with one verse of fourteen lines and ten syllables to each line. Although it is all one stanza, there are distinct groups which consist of the first eight lines and then the next six lines which contain a change of tone.

Enjambement – the sense of what's said is split between two or more lines. This helps to emphasise and draws attention to them. For example:

> Poor chap, he had this obsession with
> Triangles, so he left off two of my
> Feet.
> > *Not my best side*, U A Fanthorpe

Practice

1 Comment on the rhythm and rhyme in the first two lines of this poem by W H Auden:

> This is the night mail crossing the border,
> Bringing the cheque and the postal order,

2 Look at a poem you are studying. What can you say about its form?

Satire

Alexander Pope (1688–1744) wrote poetry in an age which began to question and challenge what had previously been considered unchallengeable.

His poem *The Rape of the Lock*, about the theft of a lock of hair, mocks the grand subject matter of epic poems and the importance they placed on what he considered to be trivial matters:

> This nymph, to the destruction of mankind,
> Nourish'd two locks, which graceful hung behind
> In equal curls ...

Language and poetic devices

Every word in a poem must work to make the whole. Poetic language makes pictures, prompts thoughts and reflections and creates moods. Look at the overall effect of language in a poem – is it economical or descriptive, flowery and sentimental, old-fashioned and formal or modern with accents and slang? Are the words used hard or soft, gentle or harsh, short or long? In addition to the type of language used, poets use particular techniques to achieve different effects. Think about the work these devices do.

Alliteration – the first sound or sounds of several words or lines are the same; e.g.

Losels, loblolly-men, louts ...
(*Toads*, Philip Larkin)

Image – word picture used to make an idea come alive. Your imagination makes your own version of the picture a poet has sketched out for you. For example:

I give you an onion.
It is a moon wrapped in brown paper.
(*Valentine*, Carol Ann Duffy)

Metaphor – not to be confused with the simile – a description of something essentially different but also similar in some way to something else. For example: *The Road Not Taken*, by Robert Frost. The whole poem compares life's choices to a branching road.

Devices – similes

A simile is a comparison between two apparently dissimilar things, often linked with 'as' or 'like':

Similes create images in the reader's mind. How effective are these examples?

- *I wandered lonely as a cloud.* (W Wordsworth)
- *What passing-bells for these who die as cattle?* (W Owen)
- *O, my Luve's like a red, red rose* (R Burns)
- *Like to the lark at break of day arising ...* (W Shakespeare)

Personification – a description of something non-human as if it were a person. For example:

> *Forest letting her hair down*
> > (*For Forest*, Grace Nichols)

Onomatopoeia – the words used sound like what they are describing. For example:

> *The stuttering rifle's rapid rattle ...*
> > (*Anthem for Doomed Youth*, Wilfred Owen)

Assonance – the same vowel sounds used in several words together create a mood or emphasise meaning. For example:

> *...the human race may with tall walls wall me*
> > (*Stepping Out*, Louis MacNeice)

Poetic Devices – Mind Map

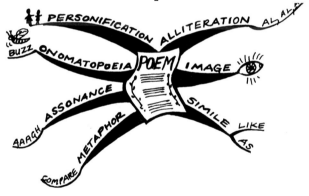

Practice

Look at a poem you are studying. What can you say about the language and devices used?

Dialect

This is the term given to non-standard English. It is characterised by the use of unusual vocabulary and grammar.

Here is an example from *Up in the Morning Early*, by Robert Burns:

> *Cauld blaws the wind frae east to west.*

What dialect is this and how can you tell? Hint: read aloud and look at the effect of the vowel sounds in *cauld, blaws* and *frae*.

Studying poems

The following poem is by Caribbean poet Grace Nichols.

Praise Song For My Mother

You were
water to me
deep and bold and fathoming
You were
moon's eye to me
full and grained and mantling
You were
sunrise to me
rise and warm and streaming
You were
the fishes red gill to me
the flame tree's spread to me
the crab's leg/the fried plantain smell
                        replenishing replenishing
Go to your wide future, you said

Make notes at the side of the poem (use colour to help clarify your thoughts), checking back to pp. 66–9 to prompt you. Here are some ideas:

- How does the title relate to content?
- Circle unusual or striking words or phrases.
- Use different colours to highlight words expressing different emotions; e.g. yellow for happiness and blue for grief.
- Highlight repetition.
- Pick out natural images.
- Look at the way the poem ends. Has it developed or changed?

Devices – metaphors

A metaphor is a description of something essentially different but also in some way similar to something else.

In *Praise Song For My Mother*, Grace Nichols compares the nurturing influence of her mother to water, the moon and sunrise. She attributes qualities to each element that particularly reflect what her mother meant to her. These qualities are imaginative rather than factual.

This is how you might have marked the poem:

celebration

Praise Song For My Mother
You were
water to me
deep and bold and fathoming
You were
moon's eye to me
pull and grained and mantling
You were
sunrise to me
rise and warm and streaming
You were
the fishes red gill to me
the flame tree's spread to me
the crab's leg/the fried plantain smell
replenishing replenishing
Go to your wide future, you said

rhythm
joy

natural elements

repetition
line stands out

sense of place – childhood memories

longer verse – builds up

generosity – giving

Here are some additional points:

- The repetition of 'You were ... to me', and the use of three words each to describe water, the moon and the sun add rhythm and form.
- The longer last stanza ends with memories of the mother giving; being everything to her daughter; and letting her go to live her own life.

Practice

1 Which parts of the poem did you most like/dislike/find difficult?
2 Make a Mind Map of this poem.

Comment effectively

You will gain marks for the effective use of terms such as **simile** and **metaphor**.

Be careful not to just pin labels on words – comment on the particular feature of language you are referring to, e.g: instead of saying 'The poet says her mother was like water. This is a metaphor', say, for example, 'I find the metaphor of water effective because it suggests that the mother ...'

Applying what you know

Remember

Remember me when I am gone away,
Gone far away into the silent land;
When you can no more hold me by the hand,
Nor I half turn to go yet turning stay.
Remember me when no more day by day
You tell me of our future that you planned:
Only remember me; you understand
It will be late to counsel then or pray.
Yet if you should forget me for a while
And afterwards remember, do not grieve:
For if the darkness and corruption leave
A vestige of the thoughts that once I had,
Better by far you should forget and smile
Than that you should remember and be sad.
         (Christina Rossetti)

Look at these points and underline/circle/make notes on the poem with coloured pens. Think about and answer the questions.

(If you've looked at pages 70 and 71 you'll find this task easier.)

- What is the poem about?
- What is the poet worried about (purpose)?
- Underline/circle unusual or striking words or phrases – then pause to think about why.
- Pick out the pairs of opposites – what effect do they have?
- Highlight repetition – what is its purpose?
- Look at the way the poem ends – decide how it has developed or changed.
- Old-fashioned words and phrases – when was the poem written?
- Look at the rhyming scheme of *Remember* – what effect does it have?
- Identify the poet's use of enjambement – what effect does it have?

Now highlight the facts from this list

- The title of this poem is a request/command/question/appeal.
- This poem is/is not a sonnet.
- There are 9/10/11/12 syllables to each line.
- The language used is simple/complex.

Comparing poems

Look back to pages 70 and 72 and read the two poems *Praise Song For My Mother* and *Remember* again. Note any new thoughts or ideas you have. You might find it useful to make large photocopies that you can write on. Look at what similarities and differences there are.

How do these poems compare?

- Try thinking about how the theme of love is dealt with – one poem deals with love for a mother and the other for a lover.
- How strongly is the love expressed – how precious is it and how is it viewed from life and perhaps death?
- How is the separation between the subject and the writer expressed?
- What sort of relationship do the poets have with the subject of their poems?
- Look at the use of imagery in both poems.
- Pick out three things that show the poems were written in different centuries.
- Describe the overall tone of these poems – e.g. sentimental/fond/worried/ insecure/glad/happy/miserable/reflective/brooding.
- How does the form of each poem back up its themes and purpose?
- What do the poems tell us about the different worlds and cultures of the poets?
- Look at and comment on the way each poem ends – what similarity is there between the two women's reactions?
- Discuss with a partner which of the two poems you prefer and why.
- Which poet would you most like to meet?

Word order

Samuel Taylor Coleridge once said that poetry is 'the best words in the best order'.

In *Kubla Khan* his words create images of a mystical and exotic land. It begins with:

In Xanadu did Kubla Khan
A stately pleasure-dome decree

If instead he had written:

Did Kubla Khan in Xanadu
Decree a stately pleasure-dome

what effect would the changed word order have had on the poem?

Practice

Similarities and differences

1 Record here key words which summarise three similarities and three differences between the poems.

Similar because?	Different because?
1	1
2	2
3	3

2 Use these words as a beginning for a Mind Map.

3 A television programme about modern women poets is planned. Suggest four visual images for each poem (which could be still pictures, moving film or video) to be shown on screen while the poems are being read. Discuss with a partner some of the images or settings which would enhance the meaning of the poems and help viewers understand them in more depth.

Before you finish this topic, ask yourself if you can:

- read, talk and write about poems written before and during this century;
- identify – and write about – similarities and differences between two poems with a similar subject.

Poetic conversations

If you have time to look them up, compare the presentation of conversations in Christina Rossetti's *Uphill* with U A Fanthorpe's *You Will Be Hearing From Us Shortly*.

Rossetti's poem is written as a series of questions. She is answered reassuringly by another voice.

U A Fanthorpe's poem supplies the questions asked at an interview, and gives the interviewer's unenthusiastic responses to the interviewee's unwritten, yet clearly stated, answers.

Poetry quiz

Which word?

Which word describes:

(a) a poem of 14 lines with a formal rhyming scheme (ode/sonnet/epic)?

(b) a poem written to lament the dead (lyric/sonnet/elegy)?

(c) a verse (narrative/stanza/lines)?

(d) the ordering of words or line endings to echo pleasing sounds (rhythm/rhyme/rhyming scheme)?

(e) the feeling of movement created by the balance between stressed and unstressed syllables (rhythm/rhyme/rhyming scheme)?

Spring, summer, autumn, winter

Which season of the year do you think the poet is thinking of from these extracts? Which words or phrases support your view?

(a) *Season of mists and mellow fruitfulness,*
Close bosom-friend of the maturing sun   (J Keats)

(b) *What is all this juice and all this joy?*
A strain of the earth's sweet being in the beginning
            In Eden garden.   (G M Hopkins)

Poetry terms

What words describe:

(a) the repetition of a sound or sounds at the beginnings of words?

(b) a comparison of two things which are different yet similar in some important way, often linked with 'as' or 'like'?

(c) a description of something as if it is essentially different but also in some way similar to something else?

(d) a pair of rhyming lines, often used at the end of a poem?

Answers

Which word?
(a) sonnet
(b) elegy
(c) stanza
(d) rhyme
(e) rhythm

Spring, summer, autumn, winter
(a) autumn; mists, mellow, fruitfulness, maturing
(b) spring; juice, joy beginning

Poetry terms
(a) alliteration
(b) simile
(c) metaphor
(d) rhyming couplet

Drafting, Proofreading and the Exam 6

Coverage: drafting and proofreading; sequencing and paragraphing; punctuation; spelling; commonly confused words.

Improving a first draft

Even professional writers write a 'first draft', then put it aside for a while. When they read it again they can see how it can be improved.

Proofreading comes after redrafting. It means looking for 'mechanical' errors – as in the grid below. To identify your weaknesses, check several pages of your **marked** written work. Whenever you find a mistake of the kind listed, make a mark in pencil. Total your mistakes to see where you need to focus.

Mistakes made	How often	Total
Capitals omitted for 'I', names or new sentences		
Commas used where there should be a new sentence		
Apostrophes of ownership (e.g. boy's/boys')		
Contractions (e.g. don't, can't, didn't)		
Word confusions (e.g. their/there; accept/except)		
Misuse of ible/able/uble (e.g. possible/impassable)		
Single/double letter spellings (e.g. access)		
Plurals misspelt (e.g. tomatoes, daisies)		
Other spellings		
Awkward word order		

Sequencing and paragraphing

Sequencing is putting ideas – and therefore sentences and paragraphs – in order. Paragraphing divides your writing into manageable sections. Begin a new paragraph at every major step forward in your sequence of ideas or events.

Paragraphing is easy if you Mind Map an essay or story plan and number the branches in order. One branch (or in longer pieces, one sub-branch) equals one paragraph.

Practice

Correct the passage below: (a) make one change to the paragraph order; (b) make one change to the sentence order in the second paragraph; (c) in the third paragraph make two changes to the word order and one change each to the grammar, spelling and punctuation. A corrected version appears on p. 95.

The Edinburgh Fringe

The Fringe includes theatre, stand-up comedy, all kinds of music, art exhibitions, poetry, and street performers ranging from fire-jugglers to human statues who only move when given a coin.

Performers come from all over the world, and so do thousands of tourists and arts enthusiasts to see them. The Edinburgh Fringe is an arts festival that takes place in Scotland's capital for three weeks in August. For three weeks the city is full to bursting point.

With, at over 150 venues, over a thousand shows taking place, its difficult to choose what to go to. Some people relies on being handed, on the street, interesting flyers, others scan the Fringe Programme and read the daily reveiws.

Paragraph links

Ordering paragraphs is like climbing. You have to plan where you're going and how you're going to get there. You can't just leap from one hold – or idea – to another.

Aim for a progression of ideas, so that readers can follow your thinking.

It may be helpful to 'signpost' connections between paragraphs by opening them with appropriate links; e.g.: 'Despite this', 'On the other hand', 'As a result', 'In addition'.

Punctuation (1)

Commas and full stops

A common mistake is using a comma in place of a full stop and capital. Consider:

Sally ran to the phone.

This is a sentence because it has a subject (Sally) and an active verb (ran). 'Sally ran' is a sentence, but 'to the phone' is not. Try

Sally ran to the phone, it stopped ringing as she reached it.

This is wrong. You could write: 'Sally ran to the phone. It stopped ringing as she reached it.' Or: 'Sally ran to the phone, but it stopped ringing as she reached it.'

Commas, dashes and clauses

Commas divide parts of a sentence – clauses – to make the sense clear:

I asked Dave, who works in a garage.

Without the comma, this could mean 'Dave who works in a garage, not Dave the plumber.' A separate clause mid-sentence can also be divided off by commas:

The car, poised on the edge of the cliff, toppled over at that moment.

Read the sentence, first with the commas, then without. What's the difference?

Dashes can be used for dramatic effect, or to make a break in the flow of sense:

The young man – he might have been 15 – turned to face me.

Link words

These connect clauses, or start sentences, to smooth the flow and prepare readers for what is to come. They are useful in persuasive writing. They include:

and   because   or   but   although   which   who   whom   however nevertheless   despite   in addition   moreover.

Short sentences without link words can be used for dramatic effect, but they may sound jerky: 'I like tea. Sometimes I drink coffee. It helps me stay awake.'

Capitals

Names – of places, people, makes of cars, football teams, etc. – begin with a capital letter. Giving something a capital makes it more **specific**. The word 'dog' doesn't need a capital, but your pet poodle Fifi does! Likewise, it's 'My **mum** doesn't like housework,' but 'I think **Mum** prefers sleeping.'

Question marks and exclamation marks

Is the following right or wrong?

He asked if I wanted it with chips.

This is correct. There's no question mark, because the question is reported. But you would write, 'Do you want it with chips or without?'

Normally an exclamation mark only goes after an exclamation – usually a few words spoken with feeling, often an order:

Come here! You idiot! Oi! Get out!

However, some 'questions' get an exclamation mark; e.g. 'Who do you think you are!'

Look for examples of all these punctuation marks in good books. Check your own work for mistakes in using them.

Acronyms

Acronyms are pronounceable words made up of initials. Some become so well known that people forget their origins. Did you know the ones below?

NATO (Nato): North Atlantic Treaty Organization

UNESCO (Unesco): United Nations Educational, Scientific and Cultural Organization

Radar: Radio Detection and Ranging

Scuba: Self-Contained Underwater Breathing Apparatus

Ernie: Electronic Random Number Indicator Equipment

Punctuation (2)

Colons and semicolons (: ;)

Colons show consequences. Using one is like blowing a little trumpet to announce someone or something:

Here's what we took with us: one fork, one spoon and a teabag.

It turned out I'd wasted my time: she'd already left.

Semicolons are stronger than commas but weaker than full stops. They are useful to divide two balanced halves of a sentence, in place of 'but':

Some people hate haggis; personally I adore it.

Apostrophes

Some correct uses of apostrophes:

she's, you'd, I'd, didn't, couldn't, wouldn't, can't (to show something's been left out, but note spelling of won't – will not).

The teacher's hair stood on end. The pupils' work had gone (one teacher, two or more pupils).

Never insert an apostrophe in a plural: potatoes, bananas, menus – none of these need apostrophes.

Colons and semicolons

Colons and semicolons are often used together. Colons are useful before quotations, especially long ones or any that you start on a new line, like this:

To be or not to be ...

Semicolons are useful in lists in which some items need commas or 'and':

You need: a bowl; a frying pan, preferably non-stick; eggs, milk and flour; and a large appetite.

Catastrophic apostrophes

Apostrophes are often misused, even in print.

There are two correct uses: (1) when something has been left out – e.g. *hasn't* (has not); (2) to show possession – e.g. *the dog's bowl* (one dog), or *the dogs' bowl* (two or more dogs). Here *dog* is a **noun**.

Do not add an apostrophe to *its* (a **possessive pronoun**, like *his, her* and *their*), or to plurals of nouns (e.g. *potatoes*).

Dialogue

Punctuate as follows:

> *'What colour's your lipstick?' asked Sonia.*
> *'Plum, I think,' murmured Jane.*
> *'Taste nice?'*
> *'Not bad.'*

For more complicated cases, see how it's done in any good novel.

Quotations

Present long quotations as separate blocks of text without quotation marks. Shorter quotations are presented like this:

> *Lady Macbeth's line, 'Unsex me here!' is shocking.*

For quotations within a quotation, use double quotation-marks:

> *Amir interrupted: 'But when Romeo says "A rose by any other name would smell as sweet", he's not talking about gardening.'*

Practice

1 Rewrite a short passage from a modern play as dialogue, using 'he said', 'she said', etc.

2 Turn the following 'reported speech' into dialogue, with speech marks:
   Dave asked Rita if she'd go out with him. She told him she would if Louise didn't mind.

Dialogue: the finer points

Vary how you present dialogue in a story or personal account. Don't end every speech with 'he/she said'. Nor do you have to use the speaker's name each time, so long as it is clear who is speaking.

For example, you could try:

> *Bond strode up to the bar. 'Orange juice, Charles,' he announced.*
>
> *'On its own, sir?' the barman queried doubtfully.*
>
> *'Yes, Charles – like me.'*

Spelling (1)

Spelling rules

Some spellings can be remembered by little rhymes, or by conjuring up mental pictures to help you remember. These memory techniques, called **mnemonics**, are discussed on the next page.

Pronunciation is also helpful, often providing the key to whether or not a word has a double letter in the middle:

tinny/tiny

spinner/spiny

dinner/diner

bitter/biter.

It can also help you tell whether a word has an 'e' on the end or not:

dot/dote

spat/spate

tot/tote

writ/write

mat/mate.

A lot of these words turn into 'ing' words in a consistent way. Those without the 'e' usually double their last letter; those with an 'e' don't: dotting/doting, totting/toting, matting/mating.

Spelling adverbs

An adverb describes how something is done. For those formed from adjectives ending in *y*, add *il* before the *y*; e.g. *hastily, tastily, wearily.*

For adjectives ending in *l* add *ly*; e.g. *beautifully, carefully, gratefully.*

For those ending in *ic*, add *ally*; e.g. *historically, frantically, scientifically.* But note that *public* becomes *publicly.*

For those ending in *ible* or *able*, drop the e and add *ly*; e.g. *audibly, memorably.*

Mnemonics

Mnemonics (from Mnemosyne, the Greek goddess of memory) are very useful in spelling, particularly if you make up your own. Probably the best-known is:

I before E, except after C, but only when the sound is EE.

Think of words like:

brief, belief, chief, thief, mischief, siege

receipt, receive, deceive, ceiling (after C)

weir, their, weight, height (no 'ee' sound).

Mental pictures (draw them if it helps) can also be useful, especially if they're striking, absurd or funny. You might combine them with a sentence. For example you might remember 'assessment' by saying 'I mustn't make an ass of myself in my assessment,' and picturing someone with an ass's head. Your own mnemonics will work best.

Able, ible, uble

No, it's not a witches' incantation, it's a group of commonly confused word endings. How confident are you about these:

comfortable, suitable, forgivable, fashionable, believable, passable, inedible,

indelible, incredible, horrible, indefensible, forcible, possible, soluble, voluble?

Improve your spelling

Nobody gets an 'A' just for good spelling, but you can lose marks for poor spelling. Here's a way to improve your spelling.

From your exercise books, copy the correct spellings of words you have got wrong more than once. Write them individually, in large print, on cards. Stick the cards round your room.

This will work even better if you add pictures to help your memory.

Spelling (2)

Groupings

Spelling groupings are also worth bearing in mind. When you look at the spellings corrected in your written work, see if they fit into categories, such as:

bought, brought, drought, throughout

caught, fraught, haughty

rough, tough, enough.

These can also be turned into mnemonics.

Spellchecks

Computer spellcheckers will help you to get your spellings right. But don't let it make you lazy. You won't be able to use them in the exam, and there are lots of other occasions in life when you'll have to rely on memory.

Get to know exactly what your spellcheck does. It won't catch simple word confusions (such as **bought** and **brought**), and it will probably offer you silly alternatives to names – such as 'Emu' for 'Emma'. Which of the following errors will your spellcheck catch?

> A police offer came to are house the other day. He asked who's car was parked on the rode out side. It had too bold tires and oil dripping out of the breaks. My farther came to the door to see watt the matter was. Their was no use trying to deny it: it was hiss.

Try it out and see if you were right.

1 George Bernard Shaw made up the word ghoti. It spells 'fish'. Can you see how? Answer: 'f' as in 'enough', 'i' as in 'women', and 'sh' as in 'lotion'. Try to make up similar words to remind yourself of spellings.
2 Make a list of words you've got wrong more than once in marked work. Learn them.

Commonly confused words

Mnemonics

These memory techniques will help you here. Here are some to start you off – but making up your own is more effective.

> Mark my eXcess baggage with an X.
> The ambassador's parrot was too discrEEt to scrEEch.
> Not tHERE – HERE!
> I was LED into the SHED.
> I ACCidentally used my ACCess card.
> THOR was ROUGH but THOROUGH.

Commonly confused words

accept/except	I **accept** your offer – **except** that I insist on paying.
access/excess	There's no **access** to anyone with **excess** baggage.
affect/effect	The rain won't **affect** us indoors. You'll spoil the **effect**.
complement/ compliment	The flavours **complement** each other: my **compliments** to the chef!
discreet/discrete	Diplomats are **discreet**. Wales isn't England – it has a **discrete** identity.
knew/new	I **knew** you'd found someone **new**.
lead/led	You now **lead** me where I once **led** you.
licence/license	A driving **licence** (noun) doesn't **license** (verb) you to kill.
lose/loose	I'd hate to **lose** my **loose** change.
passed/past	I **passed** (verb) a ghost from my **past** (noun) on the way here.
practise/practice	Try to **practise** every day – **practice** makes perfect.
principal/ principle	The new school **principal** has no **principles**.
quiet/quite	Do be **quiet** – you're making me **quite** ill.
stationary/ stationery	The train is **stationary**. A **stationery** shop sells paper.
there/their/ they're	Look over **there** and you'll see **their** clothes: **they're** swimming.
thorough/ through	The police were **thorough** in going **through** my drawers.
to/too/two	Thanks **to** you it's **too** late to find a room with **two** beds.
who's/whose	**Who's** the culprit? **Whose** muddy boots are these?
your/you're	**Your** brother's a criminal, and **you're** almost as bad.

Tackling the exam

First and foremost, stay calm and don't panic. Just remember that in English whatever you have to say is valid and worth writing. If you've worked through these notes, the best thing you can do the night before the exam is to have an early night and get plenty of rest. Wake up thinking of the exam as a chance to show off what you know!

Equipment

Black, blue and coloured pens, pencils and sharpener, rubber, watch – be sure it all works.

Preparation

• Listen carefully to the instructions.

• Make sure you fill in your name, candidate number etc.

• Read the paper carefully.

• Be sure you know how many questions you have to answer – from which sections – and which ones are compulsory.

• Check, and read again if necessary to make sure you are right.

• Plan how long you can spend on each question – too many students either misunderstand the number of questions they are required to answer, or run out of time.

• Allow more time for questions that carry more marks.

• Allow ten minutes at the end for checking work and correcting mistakes.

Standard and non-standard English

• Standard English: formal, as in BBC news – widely understood. Spoken in any accent. Write exam essays in standard English.

• Non-standard English: informal – used for chatting with friends, etc. Can include differences in vocabulary and grammar from standard English (e.g. slang, dialect).

• Non-standard English is not wrong, but it is inappropriate for formal use. You could write story dialogue in this style, but keep it easy to understand.

Answering questions

Before you start answering a question, make sure you understand it, especially if it's in parts. Mind Map what you want to include, and add new ideas as you go along.

- Write quickly and clearly.
- Take extra care over spelling and punctuation.
- Keep a close eye on time – don't run over the time allocated to each question.
- When you finish answering a question, re-read the question to make sure you've answered all the parts – ask yourself, have I done what I was asked to do?
- Make sure the answer pages are in the right order, numbered, with your name on each.

Good luck!

Exam – Mind Map

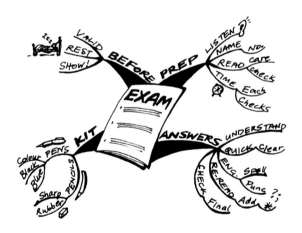

The English exam – writing

You'll be tested separately on reading and writing. A choice of writing questions, based on the reading part of the exam, will test your ability to:

- argue, persuade, instruct;
- inform, explain, describe.

You may be given a context; e.g. 'magazine article', or 'letter to a newspaper'. Suit your style and vocabulary to the purpose and context.

The English exam – reading

You'll be asked to read a piece of non-fiction. You may have to comment on content, fact and opinion, and style (or how it 'achieves its effects'). You may be asked to compare it with another piece.

Consider the author's intention; e.g. to entertain, or to persuade. You will get marks for showing how this is achieved.

Remember that non-fiction can use many of the techniques of fiction; e.g. imagery.

Beginnings

Beginnings – in fiction or non-fiction – should capture attention, supply basic information, arouse curiosity and suggest what is to come. How does the following opening do this?

As captain of a team that hadn't scored all season, Sammy 'the Bull' Thomas had reason to despair. Yet as he surveyed the scene before him, he felt that Walton City's luck was on the turn.

Make readers want to continue

Fiction: give characters traits readers can **identify** with. Describe scenes so readers can **imagine** them. Include **conflict**, **confusion** or **mystery**, so that outcome is uncertain and readers want to know what happens.

Non-fiction: back up **facts** and **arguments** with an appeal to **imagination** and **emotion**. You can use many of the techniques used in fiction – e.g. metaphor, simile, scene-setting (*A jungle classroom: light filters through the leaves of giant ferns ...*).

Endings

How you end a piece of exam writing depends on your purpose.

Generally, in **non-fiction** you should sum up your arguments in a short, punchy conclusion. In **fiction** you should give the reader a sense of completion, and perhaps a sense that the story itself will continue beyond your last page.

Avoid simply repeating what you have already said, or using a clichéd ending such as: *And then I woke up. It had all been a dream!*

Model answer

Here is an example of an A-grade exam essay, with its plan. The reference numbers in the essay (e.g. in the first paragraph) refer to what's good about the essay. See the list of points at the end.

How is kingship presented in *Macbeth*?

Plan

1 Context: Divine Right, social order, regicide
2 Malcolm's list of graces, and test
3 Edward
4 Duncan and Malcolm
5 Macbeth and Banquo
6 Imagery: owl/falcon; strangled sun

In Shakespeare's time, most people believed in the Divine Right of kings: kings were thought to be appointed by God to preserve the social order. Thus, Duncan's murder is a crime against God and society,[1] which is why Macduff says, on discovering it:

> *Confusion now hath made his masterpiece!*
> *Most sacrilegious murder hath broke ope*
> *The Lord's anointed temple.*[2]

Here confusion (chaos) and murder are personified. Confusion destroys the order created by God. The temple is the body of Duncan, anointed at his coronation.[3]

In Act 4, scene 3, when Malcolm tests Macduff's loyalty by pretending to be unfit to be king, he lists what he sees as the 'king-becoming graces'. These are justice, truthfulness, moderation, stability, generosity, perseverance, mercy, humility, devotion, patience, courage, and strength of character.[4] This gives us a yardstick against which to measure the play's three kings – Duncan, Malcolm and Macbeth.

A fourth king, the English Edward, does not actually appear in the play, but his powers of healing and prophecy are described. Shakespeare probably included this description partly to flatter James I, who thought he had inherited these powers spiritually from Edward.[5] It is not essential to the play, and allows the pace of the scene to sag.[6] However, it does form a contrast to Macbeth, who brings sickness to his country, and to the evil, 'equivocating' prophecies of the Witches.

Duncan certainly has kingly 'graces'.[7] He appreciates those who fight on his side, and he has the humility to thank them. He also shows justice in punishing treachery and rewarding noble deeds.

Even Macbeth admits that Duncan has been an excellent king, 'clear in his great office'.[8]

If Duncan has faults, they are that he is too trusting, and does not distribute rewards fairly. He builds 'An absolute trust' on the treacherous Thane of Cawdor and is similarly taken in by Macbeth, and he rewards only Macbeth, not the equally deserving Banquo.

Malcolm shows similar virtues to his father. The link between them is also made clear by imagery. Both talk about 'planting' good men and good deeds, so that they may grow healthily.[9] However, Malcolm is less trusting, as is shown by his testing of Macduff's loyalty, and in his final speech he makes his 'thanes and kinsmen' earls, rather than just honouring one man.

Macbeth does not seem to have the first two vices that Malcolm accuses himself of – lustfulness and greed, but he is solely concerned with his own power, not his country's well-being. He becomes a hated tyrant, who keeps spies in every household and rules by fear. His cruelty is shown by his massacre of Macduff's family.[10]

Macbeth is essentially a soldier, not a king. He fears Banquo's 'royalty of nature' not only because Banquo might expose him, and because the Witches have predicted that Banquo's descendants will be kings (James I was one of them), but because he knows that Banquo would make a better king than him.[11] In murdering Duncan, he is like the owl that the Old Man says has killed a falcon (a royal bird), or like night strangling the sun, another symbol of kingship (Act 2, scene 4).[12]

In Act 5, scene 2, Angus compares Macbeth to a 'dwarfish thief' who feels his kingship 'Hang loose about him, like a giant's robe'.[13] He is unworthy of his stolen throne. When he is replaced by Malcolm, a worthy king, the social order is restored.[14]

What's so good about it?

1 Relevant use of historical context.
2 Good use of quote to back up point.
3 Understanding of text.
4 Gives a sound basis for assessment and shows understanding.
5 Relevant background knowledge.
6 Ability to evaluate.
7 Refers back to an earlier point.
8 Good use of quote.
9 Understanding of kingship, and imagery.
10 Good use of an example.
11 Interesting interpretation.
12 Grasp of relevant imagery.
13 Good, selective use of quoted image.
14 Good conclusion, drawing ideas together without waffle.

Drafting quiz

Order your ideas

Below are paragraph ideas for an essay: 'The world is getting steadily worse – discuss'. Order them in a logical progression:

(a) Democracy, human rights, modern medicine.
(b) Ancient times: no pollution, more starvation and disease.
(c) Crime and pollution.
(d) World better for some, but expectations higher.
(e) People think of the 'old days' as better.
(f) Population explosion.

Punctuation

1 What punctuation mark can be used to introduce a list?
2 Which, if any, of these are correctly punctuated?

    (a) Jason ran into the house, the money was gone.
    (b) Don't lie to me – I know you took it.
    (c) The bag lay on the floor, it's contents strewn around.
3 How do you form adverbs from adjectives ending in *y*?

Writing

What is the purpose of each of the following sentences?

(a) Avoid the temptation to swim: the river is crocodile-infested.
(b) The proposed new road would gouge a gaping wound in an unspoilt hillside.
(c) Connect the brown wire to the live terminal (L), the blue to the neutral (N), and the yellow and green to the earth (E).
(d) We offer unequalled value, years of expertise, and a full ten-year guarantee.

Answer to sequencing exercise

The Edinburgh Fringe – see page 79

The Edinburgh Fringe is an arts festival that takes place in Scotland's capital for three weeks in August. Performers come from all over the world, and so do thousands of tourists and arts enthusiasts to see them. For three weeks the city is full to bursting point.

The Fringe includes theatre, stand-up comedy, all kinds of music, art exhibitions, poetry, and street performers ranging from fire-jugglers to human statues who only move when given a coin.

With over a thousand shows taking place, at over 150 venues, it's difficult to choose what to go to. Some people rely on being handed interesting flyers on the street. Others scan the Fringe Programme and read the daily reviews.

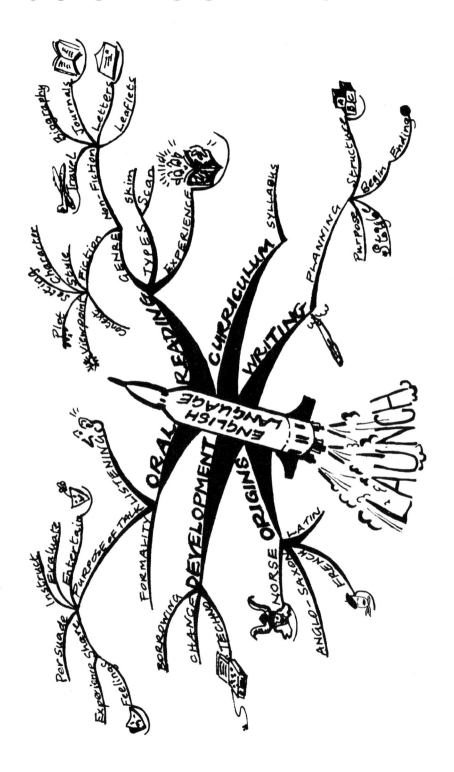